Ringless
NOT
WORTHLESS

Thriving as a Single LDS Woman

ELISA BLACK

Copyright ©2023 by Elisa Black

All rights reserved. No part of this book may be reproduced in part or whole in any form or by any means without the written permission of the publisher, except for the use of brief quotations. This book is not an official publication of The Church of Jesus Christ of Latter-Day Saints.

To request permissions, contact the publisher at www.ringlessnotworthless.com

ISBN 979-8-9875831-0-4

Manufactured in the United States of America

Contents

Acknowledgments..4
Special Thanks... 6
Introduction 7

Part One: Know Thyself

1. "What's wrong with me?" 11
2. The Authentic You 27
3. Self-Love 41

Part Two: Moving Forward

4. Expectations ………………....……………………..60
5. Navigating Adulthood …………………………………...77
6. Progress When You Feel Stuck …………………………..91

Part Three: Relationships

7. Support And Boundaries ………………………………...113
8. Connecting With God …………………………………...131
9. Church Culture ………………………………………...146
10. Dating ………………………………………………...165

Part Four: Personal Peace

11. Overcoming Fears …………………………………...184
12. Finding Hope ………………………………………...206

Acknowledgments

There are many people that have helped shape and influence me into the person I am today. This book is a compilation of many of the lessons I have learned from incredible people that I have been privileged to associate with.

In creating this book, there are people I especially want to acknowledge. First, would be my sister Malorie. She and I have been on this single woman journey together for what feels like a very long time. Even though she is younger than me, she has greatly influenced me in everything from learning to ride a bike, to starting personal scripture study, to buying a home. So many of the ideas for this book have come from our many discussions and chats as we have figured this unexpected life out together. Thank you.

Next, I want to acknowledge the women who contributed to the writing of this book. At the end of each chapter is a section written by another woman who has or is going through being single longer than expected. There are so many incredible women whose stories should be told, and I feel privileged to have been able to connect with these women and for their ability to seek and follow revelation as they added to this book.

I also want to thank the members of the many single wards I have attended, as well as every woman that has ever been my roommate. I have learned so much by interacting and living with you. Lessons at church have been edifying and helpful and your examples have blessed my life.

Then there are those who made it possible for this project to go from bits of stories into an actual, publishable work. Paula Jean Ferri was a connection made through social media who helped me learn how to get a book off the ground. She led me to the phenomenal team at Eschler Editing. They have helped with editing and the book cover design. Beverly Yellowhorse is also part of this important editing team – this book wouldn't have ever happened if it weren't for her help. Also, to my prereaders who helped during the very early stages of this book – thank you.

I also want to thank everyone who responded to my social media polls for book title and cover designs. This book was first called "Parting the Red Sea" then "Marriage is Not the Answer" then "A Singular Success" before finally landing on what it is today, and that couldn't have happened without the input and ideas of many of my friends, family, and followers. Thanks to each one of you!

And lastly a thank you to my assistant Monterey Nelson. She has done many odd jobs and completed a whole bunch of research for us to make this project go from a book to even more resources to help women looking for their place in God's plan. Thank you!

Special Thanks

Special thanks to these individuals for believing in this book and in me, enough to help get it off the ground and into the hands of those who need it. I super appreciate you!

Bronze Sponsors
Rachel Melton
Mckenzie Leach
Alyson Walker
Brent Giles
Cynthia Montrose
Rachel Augustus
Sean and Aubrie VanBlack
Sara Ricords
Ana Johnson
Shonay Patterson
Jacqueline Loos
Kelsie Albert
Mckenzie Meyer
Kelsey Munson

Silver Sponsors
Malorie Black
Anonymous
Monica and Tony Nelson
Scott Asbell

Gold Sponsors
Anonymous

Diamond Sponsors
William and Audrey Black
Joel Yellowhorse

Introduction

I used to think that if I could prove that I couldn't function well without a husband, then God would answer my prayers. I was a hot, depressed mess, always crying and praying that I would get married. I didn't try and fix things because I wanted getting married to be my answer.

Years went by and... it didn't work.

Chances are, if you picked up this book, you're an awesome Latter-day Saint female who somehow isn't married. No one prepared you to be single this long. Every Young Women's class you went to was about preparing for marriage or kids. Your parents probably were married at your age or earlier. Most of your friends are already married or close to it. Maybe you're getting desperate.

One night I went to pick up a friend who worked at the MTC. As I sat outside the gate, feeling depressed, a voice in my mind said clearly to me: "Why worry about being single. Don't you know you are going to be with your husband for *eternity*?"

I was blown away that God would tell me something like that. Shouldn't I desperately be trying to get married??? Wasn't that what God wanted me to do? And here He was, telling me not to worry about it because I was going to be with my husband for forever. I knew then that no matter how long it would take, I would have a husband, and we'd be together for eternity.

That experience happened about 10 years ago. I have heard that if you spend 10,000 hours on something, you are an expert at it. Well, I have spent far more than 10,000 hours as a single adult, with most of those years spent in Provo Utah. I know firsthand what many women of the church are experiencing. During these years, I have also started three businesses, been a foster mom, and represented the USA for the International Women's Conference in Dubai. I own homes throughout the country, I have served a mission, graduated from college, performed in a number of bands, and served in almost every calling that exists in YSA wards. I tell you these things to let you know that if it is possible for me to go from depressed to thriving, it is possible for you. My goal with this book is to give hope, encouragement, and show you through my experience how to overcome the things that make being a single woman in The Church of Jesus Christ of Latter-Day Saints so hard. Each chapter covers a specific trial that comes with being single. I will give you tools and examples of how I have overcome these things. Then at the end of each chapter there's another awesome single woman who shares her insights. As we share all of our experiences, I hope you see you are not alone in feeling incomplete, unloved, and unfulfilled. I have felt all those things to the point where I thought I would explode. But then like all of the women in this book, you can go from that negative state to finding peace and joy in your life.

Perhaps God *blessed* me to be single this long to learn these hard things, and how to overcome them, so I could share what I have learned with you. But whatever the purpose, I know God lives, I know God loves me just as much as my friends who are married, and I know he has a work and a plan for me. You're a noble daughter of a Heavenly Father as well, and it's time to stop hiding your light because you are fearful it will scare away potential suitors, or that you aren't good enough to shine. Those things simply aren't true.

You *deserve* to be happy, enjoy your life, and receive all the great blessings that God has to offer you, right now, as a single person. You're a rockstar, and God needs you to be your best self. Nothing about you or your life is a mistake. It may seem crazy to believe that marriage is not the answer to happiness, but parting the red sea also seemed crazy to the Israelites. Miracles happen. God said we are to have joy (2 Ne 2:25), but he never says that is conditional on marriage. You can do this! You may be ringless, but you are far from worthless.

A Note to YSA Bishops and Their Wives

I am so grateful for the amazing bishops and their wives that I have been privileged to know over the years. As I haven't remained in one place very long over the last 12 years, I have gotten to know several.

If you are reading this book in an attempt to help understand the struggles of your ward members more, I would like to provide one specific note to you: when sharing with us, it is a lot more helpful if you focus on how *Christ* helped you through trials, rather than your spouse. I understand that your spouse was there, and that you can't imagine going through that trial without that support. But you are talking to a congregation that is doing just that- going through life's ups and downs without a spouse. Every second of every day, we have to face our trials without that support. So, when we hear "I couldn't have overcome that without my husband", it can hurt. It can make us feel like we don't have the support we need to overcome our trials, or even that we don't deserve help. Let's reinforce the truth that Christ is the source of all help and light. *He* is the one who we must turn to. *He* is the greatest source of strength and direction we have- no matter our relationship status.

Again, thank you for your service and leadership. We put a lot of trust in you and are grateful for your dedication and love.

Section 1
Know Thyself

"I believe in myself. I do not mean to say this with egotism. But I believe in my capacity and in your capacity to do good, to make some contribution to the society of which we are a part, [and] to grow and develop. ... I believe in the principle that I can make a difference in this world, be it ever so small." "President Hinckley Shares Ten Beliefs with Chamber" Church News, Jan. 31, 1998, 4.

Chapter 1
"What's wrong with me?"

"...let virtue garnish they thoughts unceasingly; then shall thy confidence wax strong in the presence of God..." D&C 121:45

When I was around 18 years old, an older cousin of mine did a workshop about being the change you want to see in the world. She was female and single, and I thought she was incredible (I still do). She said that as a 27- year-old single female, she had had to overcome the thoughts and feelings that something must be wrong with her. I thought it was crazy that she could think there was something wrong with her- she was talented, spiritual, and pretty. As I would learn during my own single journey though, it's hard *not* to assume there is something wrong with you when you remain unmarried in a world where marrying young is considered the norm.

Is there something wrong with you if you are older than your parents were when they got married, or you graduate college unmarried, or you passed the year when you assumed you would be married?

No. There is absolutely nothing wrong with you. You don't reach a certain level of spirituality, or overcome enough of your flaws, to then be worthy of marriage. All you have to do is open the scriptures to find story after story of bad things happening to good people. Life is not like Santa Claus: full of rewards for the good people, and punishment for the bad. This is a good thing. If life were that way, we wouldn't grow and learn and have the richness and complexities that life offers. We wouldn't be able to be like God one day.

You can free yourself by facing the truth that there really isn't anything 'wrong' with you. When you truly believe that about yourself, you can stop worrying about it, and live your best life.

You move from a place of fear and worry to a place of peace, even as you are 'waiting'. It helps you create your own personal identity, rather than see yourself as half a person until you are married. You are whole, unique, and your life has the potential to be absolutely incredible today if you let it.

The Root Of Negative Thoughts

It's hard to accept truths sometimes. Satan does a great job of brainwashing us into thinking all sorts of lies. Here is a list of some of the most common lies I have heard from single women (and myself) over the years:

"I'm not good enough"
"I must be 2nd rate in God's eyes"
"I don't deserve to be married"
"I must be doing something wrong"
"Is this a punishment?"
"Does God not love me?"
"I must not be worthy of love or marriage"
"I can't be trusted with children or I would have them"

Some of these thoughts start early, even in childhood. From experiences I had in middle school, I assumed that no guy would ever like me. This affected me in later years. I remember all the way back in high school, I liked this guy. One time in a single day he sat with his arm around me on the bus, sat by me at an assembly (where I kept my arms folded so he wouldn't think I wanted to hold hands), and offered me his jacket when I said I was cold (which I refused). I think maybe it was even that same day that he kissed me on the forehead. A couple days later my friend said he must like me. I thought she was crazy. Years later, looking back and reading through journals that talk about just how much the two of us hung out and texted, I can see that of course he liked me!

"What's wrong with me?"

But I couldn't see that because I had told myself for so long that no guy would ever want to be with me or go out with me.

The first time I recognized that Satan could be putting negative thoughts in my head was on my mission. I remember one morning during personal scripture study; the thought came to my mind: "Of course God listens to everyone's prayers. Well, everyone except yours". And I realized that even though that felt true, that thought wasn't coming from the Holy Ghost or God. It had to be the devil. I saw that the war on my mind was real. I needed to work on keeping evil out of my mind as much as anywhere else if I was going to survive my mission.

Battles in our minds are a big deal. Negative thoughts impact our lives more than most people realize. I believe they are Satan's number one tool for stopping women. Thoughts lead to behaviors, emotions, and habits. The thoughts we have can add to our happiness or fears, our ability to make things happen or hide away, and lead us to good or bad decisions in our lives. It all starts with our minds.

Some thoughts start out as good, but can become twisted. For example: "marriage in the temple will make me happy". Yes, this definitely can be true, and I whole heartedly expect marriage to add to my happiness. However, the act of getting married itself isn't what creates that happiness. This is so important for single - and well-married people - to understand. The act of marriage does not magically make life good. Happiness is dependent upon other factors, and the quality of your relationships and/or marriage can add to that. But do not depend on those relationships to make you happy, because that makes you believe you can't be happy until you are married. Thus, you might end up getting married too quickly (and end up in a bad marriage) or you could become frustrated and desperate because you feel you are being denied happiness when it hasn't happened yet.

Sometimes, a negative thought is pushed on you by someone else. For example, a ward friend told me that when her family members are mad at her, they say, "This is why you aren't married!" This is a very damaging thing to say. It implies that issues/sins/difficulties are the reason for not being married. This is simply not true.

There was a similar issue in Jesus' day. When the disciples saw a blind man, they asked Jesus: who sinned, this man or his parents? (John 9:2) Jesus answered, neither. Most people today don't see a family who loses a child, or fights cancer as being punished by God. Yet many still assume, including many single individuals themselves, that there is some issue or reason for why someone is still single. Like blindness, being single doesn't mean there's something wrong with you. It's just the life we have, and there are wonderful and beautiful parts to it if we choose to see it as God's plan for us.

The first step toward building that happiness is to change thoughts and mentality. Here are things that I have learned over the years to help smash negative thoughts and increase the positive ones. These ideas and tools can help with thoughts centered around marriage, but they can help with any other kind of negative thought you have as well.

Changing Negative Thoughts

The first step in making the change from negative thinking to positive thinking is **wanting to change**. This might seem weird- wouldn't everyone want to be in a more positive mental state and be happy? I can say for me personally, I have not always *wanted* to be positive and happy. I would prefer to wallow in my sorrows, pity myself, and be the victim. One of the reasons letting go of negative thoughts was so hard for me was because a small part of me liked to pity myself for those things. I went through a time where I felt like I had to cry during every nightly prayer for it to be real, authentic, passionate, and heard of God. I liked being depressed or sad to a degree: not when it was so debilitating that getting up in the morning was a major struggle, but I liked having deep feelings and indulging them. I had to decide that I wanted to be happy and positive more than I wanted to feel all this sadness. It was a gradual process, as sometimes I drifted back to just feeling all the sadness. But over time the positives replaced the negatives more and more and it got easier to find better coping mechanisms than wallowing and pity. It is hard to uproot the negative thoughts and emotions, and replace them with positive, good thoughts and emotions, especially if you have created habits like self-pity every time the word 'family' or 'marriage' comes up at church. You need to take the first step to reach a place where you honestly want to change.

The second step is **recognizing that it is happening.** With so many thoughts going through our brains, sometimes negative ones come so naturally that they can be hard to catch. Keeping a thought journal or notebook is a great way to do this. Try to write down thoughts that go through your mind throughout the day that are negative. Get them out on paper. You will probably need to do this for a couple of days to find all of them. The first time I did this, I took a little black notebook around with me, and when I noticed a negative thought, I'd write it down. It was a really enlightening experience actually- seeing what really was happening in my brain. Our brains are incredible and are in our stewardship to take care of the best we can.

Once the thought is on paper, creating a **"CBT thought record"** is the last step. I learned how to do this in therapy, but you can also Google it. To make a thought record you divide a paper into 7 columns. Then, pick a thought, feeling or situation you want to tackle. Column 1 is where you can write about the situation. Column 2 is to describe the feelings. There might be a mix of feelings that go into the situation. Column 3 is where you write the negative thoughts. Once the thought and feelings are down on paper, column 4 is to list evidence to support that thought. Why is that thought true? Sometimes the support isn't logical at all, but that's ok. Then in column 5 you write the evidence that doesn't support the thought- why that thought maybe isn't true. Column 6 is for creating a new thought, and column 7 is for writing down the new emotions that are connected to the new thought. Sometimes I start with column 3, sometimes 2, or sometimes 1. This is because sometimes I notice the way I am feeling before I realize what the thought is. When I realize I am having dark or negative feelings, sometimes I ask myself what the thought is that goes along with those feelings and my brain gives me an answer. Other times I write in my journal about my feelings, the situation, etc. until the thoughts become clearer.

Situation or trigger	Emotion or feeling	Negative automatic thought	Evidence that supports the thought	Evidence that does not support the thought	Alternative thought	Emotion or feeling
Describe who, what, when, where?	can use one word to describe an emotion; rate 0-100%	Identify one thought to work on	What facts support the truthfulness of this thought?	What experiences indicate that this thought is not completely true all of the time?	Write a new thought which takes into account the evidence for and against the original thought	How do you feel about the situation now? Rate 0-100%

The new thought doesn't have to be all sunshine and rainbows. It does have to create new emotions though. For example: my therapist and I worked on this thought: "I will never get married". I couldn't think of the evidence against that at first and so she helped me. I remember her saying that "never" is a very strong word and helped me focus on changing just that word which ultimately opened the door to creating a new thought. I first tried things like "I will get married"- just doing the opposite. But that didn't really make my feelings change. Feelings connected to thoughts are very powerful. It took me some time to find the perfect alternative thought for me. It ended up being: "I am a noble daughter of God". I'm not sure why that one gave me such new and positive emotions and felt like the opposite of "I will never get married", but I went with it. I listed all the emotions that this created for me as the last step. Then, when that negative thought tried to come back, I would replace it with "I am a noble daughter of God" and that really helped me to get rid of that unhelpful and negative thought.

 The negative thoughts will likely try to come back even after you do the thought record. This is because most likely you have created habit thinking. For example: maybe every time you interact with a guy you think is cute, you then tell yourself you've got no chance, or you're ugly, and ultimately it leads you to the thought "I will never get married". Now your brain is used to going down that path. But then you remember your new thought and start to think that thought instead; eventually you rewire your brain to go to a positive place instead of a negative one.

This does not take the place of needing therapy. If you are getting really stuck on thoughts and need help with the process of getting into positive thoughts, I highly recommend therapy. Especially if your negative thought spirals lead to anxiety or depression.

In With The Good

 As you are uprooting the negative, it is important to find ways to replace the negative with what you *do* want in your life. There are many ways you can increase positivity in your life.

Affirmations

 One of those things is to read and recite positive affirmations or goals to yourself. When I started doing this, I wasn't totally sold on the idea of just saying things out loud morning and night and believing that would make things happen in your life. I even read the book "Think and Grow Rich" and was still skeptical. But I did notice that the people around me that were unhappy and discontented with their lives were *not* doing this. So I decided to give it a try.

I didn't really think too much about it, just kept working on my goals even as I tried to remember to read my goals and affirmations morning and night. One of the things that I had written on my daily statements was that I wanted to be a speaker at a convention for financial professionals. Each time I read this, I pictured myself speaking on the main stage in front of 40,000 people. After about six months of reading my goals fairly consistently morning and night, I got a call a few days before the 2019 convention, inviting me to be a two-minute speaker for a breakout session. I could hardly believe it! It wasn't going to be *exactly* the way I pictured it as I read my goals, but I *was* going to speak at the convention, and in front of a couple thousand people. This taught me that reading goals does work.

This is so cool to me. Our minds have power. Not all of my goals have happened like I have hoped for and pictured…yet. But I have noticed that the constant feeding of positivity is there when I need it. Sometimes a negative thought will try to enter my mind, and a line from one of those affirmations will come to mind and push the negative thought away. Or when I am discouraged at work another line will be brought to my memory. I hope I will achieve great success in my relationships, in business, and every area of my life. But even if these affirmations simply help me stay in a positive, uplifted place, then it is worth it for me.

Associations

Something else that can help you change negative thoughts is to be around positive and uplifting people. The way we think about ourselves, those we interact with, and life, is contagious. Many success gurus, including motivational speaker Jim Rohn, have famously said that you are most like the five people you most associate with. If you are around people who like themselves, and respect themselves, and treat themselves well, you will do that too. Are you someone who wants to break the habit of watching TV every day? You will most likely need friends who don't watch TV every day.

Common Misconceptions

I don't deserve to have kids

One of the negative thoughts I mentioned was: "I must not be trustworthy with kids or I would have them". Please recognize that this is a major fallacy. Many people in the church do say that their husband and kids are blessings. New moms always post on social media and within days say things like: "I can't even imagine my life without my baby". Once I was talking with a friend who was getting married soon. She said, "I must be living right!" These kinds of comments and thoughts, though nice for the speaker, are hard to hear when you want those things and don't have them. That's why we feel second rate, or like there is something wrong with us or that we must not be good enough. Even though she said that, I know my friend doesn't think I am second rate. She doesn't think I am being punished by being single. She was just overwhelmed with happiness and gratitude in that moment. It is natural to think that good things come when you are living right. But just like with any trial that comes to good people, bad things in life are not because *we* are bad or second rate.

Single people are not being denied the blessing because they would ruin a husband or children. If only good, totally ready and emotionally mature people got married, there would be no divorce. If only good, totally ready and emotionally mature people could become mothers, there wouldn't be thousands of children in foster care in the US, and millions of children sold into slavery throughout the world. Please don't belittle yourself and let Satan convince you of these lies. You are good enough. Not being married and not having children never has been, nor ever will be because someone is not good enough. There is simply zero correlation between those two things.

There must be something I need to change

"What do I need to change to get married?" This one is an interesting thought. I say interesting, because it can be used in a positive uplifting way, but it can also be negative. It depends on your feelings around this thought.

A more positive way to think about it might be: "how can I attract the kind of guy I am attracted to?" This is like the exercises in Young Women where you make a list of qualities you want in a marriage partner and then ask yourself what you need to do to become the kind of person that will attract a person with those qualities. Using that kind of question as a positive motivator to increase scripture reading in your life, and exercise more, or work hard, etc., is a great thing.

Are there things we can always be working on and improving? Of course. But that is true before *and* after marriage. Marriage is not a destination. Eternity would be super long and boring in my opinion if simply getting married was the purpose of life and everything. So if that question, "what do I need to change in order to get married?" is helpful to you in becoming your best self, then great. If it isn't helpful, then don't ever think about it again.

I'm not as good as someone married before me

God doesn't intend for us to feel like we are worth less than others by not being married. And it's not just girls who deal with this. Once at church I went up to one of my guy friends who was sitting in the church foyer. We could hear another ward in a sacrament meeting, and there was a gentleman giving a talk. My friend had been listening to the talk before I came over. He said something along these lines to me: "This talk is really good. I looked in the chapel, and sure enough it's a family ward. It was too good of a talk and too spiritual to be from a guy who is still single."

"What's wrong with me?"

He was saying it like a joke, but I could tell he meant it. Labeling ourselves as not as good because of our relationship status is not an idea that comes from God. The quality of that talk has nothing to do with that man being married or single. We are not second class members because of our relationship status.

Shift Your Focus

When you accept that not being married has nothing to do with whether or not you have problems, you will most likely need to do some mental shifting. And this is a very good thing. Any time we are making positive changes, that is repentance. What a beautiful thing that is. We have the opportunity to change how we think about ourselves. Thank heavens for repentance! This also means we will need to connect with Father in Heaven to see His will for us. Maybe there are things you can only do for the Lord while you are single.

A number of years ago, when I was going through a hard time, my friend and roommate introduced me to YouTube videos done by life coach Tony Robbins. Tony is probably the most well-known life coach on the planet. He's in high demand because he's very good at what he does. He's done a lot of good for thousands - if not millions - of people with his group conventions and seminars. (If you don't know him and want to look him up, I will warn you he has no language filter.) Sometimes when I was sad, I would watch these videos with my friend and try to figure out how to live my life and get married, even with no marriage prospects in sight.

Because of doing that before bed so much, one night Tony came to me in a dream. He came to coach just me, one on one. I was telling him my troubles and why I was so sad. He then said to me: "If you're not happy now, what makes you think you will be happy when you are married?"

Marriage wasn't the magic pill I needed. I needed to figure out how to be happy on my own in order to have more of a chance at a future happy marriage. Happiness does not come *from* marriage. Your life doesn't start or end with marriage. Marriage isn't some kind of prize or award for being a good person. You are a wonderful and loved daughter of God. He cares about you and your happiness deeply. If you look closely enough, you can see His hand every day of your life. You aren't single as a punishment, or because you're not as good or as pretty or as thin, or as *anything* as anyone else. Progress for your life is not contingent upon marriage by a certain age or date. God needs His single women, and as Elder Neil L. Andersen said in the April 2021 conference: "There can be happiness in the journey of mortality even when all of our righteous hopes are not realized." You have high value and high worth today, just as you are.

Rachel W.'s Story.

Recently I've had a lot of talks with different friends and some family members about where I'm at in life. My friends and my family have been my sounding board. I used to be a very private person, but lately I've been able to open up to people about specific things and tell them how I feel. I never thought that I would open up about being single though, and the hardship that comes with that.

Over the last few years, I have really struggled with being single. I grew up always thinking that I would get married and start a family at a young age. I don't know why I thought that. I was always the shy one. I am an introvert and I would much rather sit at home on my couch watching TV than be out in a crowd of people socializing. But for some reason, when I turned 25 and wasn't married, all I could think about was, "what is wrong with me?" I started to think that I wasn't pretty enough or social enough or good enough. I thought for sure that the people who were getting married were better than me. I started to get down on myself. I've always struggled with a little bit of depression, but the older I got, and the further away from that "get married at a young age" goal that I had, the more my depression showed. My friends had to force me to go out with them.

When I graduated from college, I lived at home for a time, and made all the excuses to not go out and meet new people. I started going to a YSA ward, but I never liked going to the activities because my introverted self would shut down.

I remember talking to my mom one day and I was hurt because although she admitted I was trying, she didn't think I was "trying hard enough". But I was! All I've ever wanted was to be a wife and a mother, but the more I tried, the harder it was, and my social anxiety would kick in so much stronger!

It made no sense, so I really did start to think that something was wrong with me. Why couldn't I do it? Why couldn't I put myself out there and meet new people? Why wasn't God putting people in my life that could potentially be date material? This was hard for me. I watched so many people around me date, get engaged, and then get married. It really got me wondering what was wrong with me when the kids I babysat in my early teen years started getting married. Do you know how hard that is? One of the girls I babysat even asked me to help make the waffles for her wedding. I was happy to do it, but it was incredibly hard to see someone I babysat get married, while I was 27/28 years old, living at home with my parents and youngest brother. I went home and cried that night because I couldn't help but think that there really was something wrong with me!

At one point, I was talking to a friend and she said, "I've had a conversation with God, and I think I'm going to be single for a very long time. I might not even get married! I feel strongly about that, and I have come to peace with that." That conversation stuck in my memory, and I think I started to adopt that same mentality. I prayed, but nothing was coming, so I figured that this was God's way of telling me that I needed to start preparing to be single for a very long time.

Fast forward a couple years and I having a conversation with a dear friend of mine. We were talking about how I wasn't making friends in my new ward, I wasn't talking to my roommates, and I was just struggling. She texted me one night and told me that I needed to put forth more of an effort. This time around, she was right. I wasn't making an effort any longer. I think I had given up. Why try? Why put myself out there just to be disappointed? So, I stopped trying. But when this friend told me I needed to make an effort to put myself out there "or God can't work miracles in [my] life", it hit me hard! I had known this, and so many people over the years had told me this, but it wasn't until this time that I really took it to heart.

I got her text on the Sunday before Thanksgiving of 2019. I prayed that week harder than I had prayed in a really long time! That next Sunday someone from my ward came and sat by me and started to talk to me. Umm… God, what is this? Who is this? Why is this guy talking to me? Right then and there I knew that this was an answer to my ever-pleading prayers that week.

This guy and I became friends, went on a few dates, I got to know his roommates and other people in the ward, and my life changed. I had friends in my ward. I had adventures to go on, people who cared about me, and people I cared about. Things weren't always wonderful, but my life was good! I made friends that I loved being around, and I realized that God was answering my prayers. Over the last year I have had a lot of ups and downs because I still want to be married and have a family.

When I turned 30 years old, I had a really rough week because I never thought I would be 30 or older before I got married. It still hurts when I get rejected or when you know that the person you are falling for doesn't feel the same way. It hurts a *lot!* It makes me not want to put myself out there anymore because I know that I'm setting myself up for heartbreak again and again.

"What's wrong with me?"

I was watching *Mission Impossible* for the first time a couple weeks ago. As I was sitting there with my friends around me, I remember watching the end as Ethan is in the army hospital bed talking to his ex-wife Julia, who he still loves more than life itself. As they are talking, he apologizes for everything he put her through when they were married. She looks at him and starts talking about how she loves her life. She says things along the lines of how everything that happened helped her to know who she really is, and showed her what she was capable of. She concludes by saying that they are both exactly where they should be.

As I watched this scene, I started to cry! Not only because of the love between them, but because this was an answer to my recent prayers and my conversations with my friends. I may not be where I thought I would be, but guess what! I'm exactly where I need to be! God hasn't left me alone. God hasn't forgotten about me. I'm where I am today because of Him. Is it easy? No! It hurts so badly sometimes! There are days where I sit at the temple at midnight, bawling my eyes out, praying to God asking Him why me? Why can't I have my hopes and dreams and righteous desires come true? Trust me, I have had many conversations asking God these questions.

But then I realize... why not me? What lessons am I learning now to help someone else in the future, whether it be a friend, a family member, a future child? I know I'm getting to know myself and the strengths I have! I'm learning to serve others. I'm realizing that I'm ok being on my own sometimes. I'm finding out that I need to put the Lord first and that my scripture study and temple attendance need to be a priority in my life. I'm learning that coasting through life isn't going to get me anywhere. I'm recognizing that my friends, my family, and the Gospel of Jesus Christ are my anchors.

My co-worker has been a source of strength and one of my biggest confidants over the last year. One day I was telling her that I was struggling because I really care about someone, but it's just not going to work out like I want. She wrote back and said,

Know Thyself

"Write this down and put it somewhere you can see it every day. You need this reminder.... 'Heavenly Father has a plan for me, and I will trust Him.'" I started to cry, then wrote it on a blue sticky note and laminated it with some packing tape. It's now taped above my light switch where I can see it every time I look up from my desk and as I walk out of my room. I'm not saying this is easy, but because I have a loving Heavenly Father and a Savior who died for me and carried my sins and sorrows, I know they would never leave me alone. I know that I can trust them, and they are waiting for that perfect moment to bless me with my greatest and deepest desire.

  I think back to what Julia says in *Mission Impossible* about loving her life and finding her purpose. I felt that! If it wasn't for all the struggles I have gone through, if it wasn't for the strength I have developed, I don't know if I could know what I'm capable of. I still have so much to learn about myself and about life, but because of my situation, I am who I am today, and I wouldn't change that for the world! And no matter how hard life gets, I can say
through it all "I got this because the Lord has got me!"

Chapter 2
The Authentic You

"Trials and Tribulations tend to squeeze the artificiality out of us, leaving the essence of what we really are and clarifying what we really yearn for." - Neal A. Maxwell, *Things As They Really Are*

The Value Of Alone Time

During the pandemic of 2020, I spent a lot of time alone, as most people did. For a couple of months though, as I was transitioning to new roommates, and waiting for a foster child placement, I was *really* all alone. There were no church activities or attendance and I worked entirely from home. All I had was myself to keep me company.

There have definitely been times when I have felt lonely. However, this time of global pandemic was *not* one of those times. Part of this was that I was able to keep myself busy with work and preparing to be a foster parent. I think I also felt a connection with the rest of the world for going through the same trial.

But more than anything else, I had a chance to see that after all these years of being single, I like myself. I enjoy who I am. There were things I was doing during that difficult time purely for me and my enjoyment. I really got to see that just being me by myself is not only tolerable, but actually kind of nice. The whole house was mine, I got to do things my way; everything was on my schedule and every movie my choice.

About the time my roommate moved in, we went back to church in person for sacrament meeting. I remember some of the girls in my ward telling me that I was glowing! What could have caused me to be *glowing*? The only explanation I had was that all that alone time was really good for my soul. I needed that time to connect with myself. Life slowed down a lot too. Instead of moving constantly from one place to the next, I had time to reflect, relax, and refresh.

This experience showed me that I had reached a new level of authenticity with myself. As I have worked on stripping away the things I don't want in my life and worked on really figuring out who the real me is, I have learned things that others can learn from as well.

Take The Plunge

Figuring out who you are and loving yourself is a journey that doesn't happen overnight. It doesn't happen in one year, or after one General Conference session, or from dating the right person. For most of us, it's a lifelong pursuit. We yearn for authenticity. We despise people we think are 'fake'. The Instagram influencers we follow are the ones who seem to have figured out how to be themselves.

Part of discovering our divine potential is figuring out who we genuinely are. One of the hardest parts of this is to be patient with ourselves. It would be so nice to know ourselves perfectly right now. But that is not God's plan. He instead leads us on a journey to learn and grow to become like Him one day. As we grow our relationship with God and trust that he does know our most authentic selves, we can get to know our true selves better.

Many people today don't take the time to get to know themselves because they don't like being alone. Feeling lonely generally doesn't feel good, and most of the time we want to feel good. As single people, loneliness is something that follows us around despite our best efforts. We try to drown it out with social media, music, social activities, and TV. It can be stuffed away for a time, but eventually it sneaks back out.

Instead of always trying to fight being lonely, this single time can be a fantastic time of self-discovery and mastery, where we really get to know ourselves. This is a huge blessing. We need only choose to start working on it.

Loneliness

First, we must give ourselves permission to get to know our genuine selves by facing our loneliness. I tried so hard to avoid the feeling of loneliness that it took me a long time to realize that I was struggling with it.

Discovery

I remember one time I told my therapist that my week had mostly been really good, except that I hated going to bed. I almost always fall asleep in less than five minutes; that wasn't the issue. For some reason, after I'd spent time with family or friends, it was a huge struggle to want to go to my room and go to bed.

She asked, "Are you feeling lonely during that time?"

I quickly said, "no".

How could I feel lonely right after being with people? But then I really looked inside myself. What did loneliness feel like? I had never labeled a moment in my life as lonely. As soon as I thought: "I am lonely before bed", my brain confirmed it. I was experiencing loneliness.

Now I recognize that most people have felt lonely long before they are 27 years old. I definitely had too. It's just that without being able to label it, it's hard to deal with it. Once an emotion is labeled, it is manageable. I learned this several years ago.

I do not like driving. I didn't get my license until I was 19 years old because I didn't have a car and driving made me nervous. One day I was getting onto the freeway, hit something, and it shredded my tire. I was able to quickly get to the side of the road, but I was not going anywhere. I got on the phone and called my car insurance. While going through the annoying phone prompts, I was shaking and trying hard not to cry. I kept telling myself it was stupid to be emotional about this- it wasn't a big deal and I was fine. But that wasn't fixing how I felt. As I talked to the lady on the phone who finally answered, I was in tears. It was embarrassing. I was not in danger, and I was literally 10 minutes from my house. She had me get out of the car so I could explain the damage. Afterwards I got back into the car and hung up. I was still crying.

Then I remembered my therapy lesson about the importance of not judging your emotions or trying to make them go away without first giving them space and labeling them. I said to myself: I am scared and distressed and that's ok. About two seconds later I felt fine. How was that possible? It was because I stopped judging myself, figured out my feelings, and I was able to move on.

The line I use often is: "I'm feeling _____, and that's ok. It's a temporary feeling". That sentence works well for me in many situations and with different feelings.

Once the loneliness is labeled for me, I can do something about it. If I feel the twinge of loneliness creeping up as I leave my parents' house after Sunday dinner, I remind myself that it's ok that I am feeling lonely. The best way to get over it for me is to acknowledge that emotion, then simply get myself ready for bed right away, without letting myself focus on it too much. I also enjoy putting on a YouTube video I like, or a talk, or a book to listen to as I prep for bed.

Another time that can be difficult for me is eating dinner alone. In these moments that I find are hardest for me, I work on prepping myself in advance so that the experience is better. I plan to call a friend or do something to take my mind off of the hard time if needed, and remind myself that what I am experiencing is perfectly normal and temporary.

Be OK Being Alone

Another thing you can do to overcome feeling lonely is embrace being alone. Instead of trying to avoid it, and find distractions, just sit with yourself. Make a list of things you are grateful for, right where you are at in life. List things you like about yourself. Give yourself a hug. Be there for yourself in the same way you've been longing for someone else to be there for you. Think: if

I loved myself, what would I be doing right now? And do that. Sit in the uncomfortable feeling of loneliness and tell yourself it's temporary- you're letting yourself feel it for a moment, but then you are going to move past it into feeling peace or happiness.

Have you ever heard people say, "it happens after you give up"? I have, and I dislike that saying a lot because I don't want to ever give up. I think what it *really* means is to let go of frustration and angst. When you are living with happiness and peace in your heart, it's easier to attract what you want. That way it feels like it comes when you aren't expecting it; it just naturally slides into your life. You're able to be who you really are, inside and outside, and be at peace with that.

I have periods when I am happy and content, and other moments when I have high anxiety or loneliness. On one occasion when I was feeling content, I went out to a movie by myself. It was an opening night. When I got my ticket, I chose one near the middle, but a seat away from the next group over. As I waited, the theater seats started filling up. It was sold out. Seated next to me were two couples with their single guy friend. Since I had left a seat in between me and the group to my right, the single guy sat on that other seat. When I realized they were all together, I quickly tried to switch places, but they wouldn't let me. They were a good-natured group, and we laughed about it.

After the movie, we all walked out together. The single guy ended up asking me for my number and I thought, "Why not? I'll go on a date with him." And we did!

Things didn't go very far. But it was a good reminder that when I am in a positive non-anxious state of mind, the things I want come more easily. That's not always great news for someone who gets anxious just thinking about how anxiety affects the mind. But I keep working at it.

Singleness Does Not Equal Loneliness

Sometimes as single people, we can become self-absorbed and think we are the only ones that get lonely. That is simply not true. So many people experience loneliness in different ways.

My dad was a very young bishop. At the time they had three children, ages four and under. My mom had to keep all three in the church pew on Sundays by herself. She also had to take care of everything while dad had to stay late on Sundays for meetings, and things in the evenings during the week as well. She felt very lonely during this time.

There are people who move to new towns and feel lonely, even when they are married with kids. There are people who get divorced or have a death in the family. Loneliness is not reserved for singles.

Take courage. Your life is great. Just because you are lonely at times, doesn't mean you can't find peace and fulfillment most of the time. It's normal to have ups and downs. Just remember the difficulties and emotions you don't like aren't permanent, and they can make the happy days sweeter. We must experience the bitter to savor the sweet.

Believe In And Accept Yourself

Once you are more comfortable being alone, you can really start to get to know yourself. A lot of the next chapters will help you with ideas on how to do this. I did want to share here though, about the importance of believing in and accepting yourself in order to really find your true and authentic self.

I am a singer. In fact, I'm a good singer, better than average. This was even true from a pretty young age, but for whatever reason I had a hard time believing or accepting that for myself. I would get embarrassed and shy and only sing if I was on a stage, pretending to be a character in a musical, or if I was in a choir. I depended on other people to tell me how good I was to build my self-confidence, but still never got the guts to really push my limits or audition for solos where I would just be myself. Until I believed in me, I just couldn't do it.

I started believing and accepting myself by accident, while in the MTC in Peru. One P-day as we were waiting for our laundry, my companions and I (we were in a trio) were in our bedroom writing letters home. The window was open, and it was really easy to hear the Elders playing soccer down at the field, even though it wasn't close to our room. Being a music nerd, I admired the acoustics of the courtyard that sent the sounds up to our room so clearly. Of course, I couldn't resist. I decided to sing and see how my voice would bounce off the courtyard walls. I was very insecure about my voice, even though I was studying musical theatre in college, but I thought: what difference does it make- I'm in Peru!

The first song that came to my mind was the song "A Dream is a Wish Your Heart Makes", from Disney's *Cinderella*. I sang the first words and then stopped to listen.

To my great surprise and amazement, my own voice wasn't what came bouncing back. A male voice replied with the next words of the song as if he had been waiting for me to sing the whole time. We finished the song in a lovely and magical duet that floated perfectly around the courtyard. Then I hurried and slammed the window shut.

My companions and I laughed and laughed. Although we briefly wondered who it could have been, we soon returned to the many things we needed to do.

The next night however, as I came back up the stairs to our hall, I saw a group of sisters crowded around the window. As my companions and I neared the window, we heard a male voice finish a song and then say, "I'm waiting!". My jaw dropped.

"You have to sing again!" said one of my companions.

"We are in the MTC!" I replied.

But I eventually fell to peer pressure. It couldn't hurt to make a little music, just once more?

This went on for a couple of nights. One night as I was coming up the stairs, I heard a recorded voice singing "The Phantom of the Opera".

"Is that me?" I asked in surprise.

The sister with the recording looked at me and laughed. "No!", she said. Everyone around was laughing. Embarrassed that I had mistaken a professional recording for my voice, I hurried to leave the room.

Then she called out, "Just kidding, yes, it is you!"

I didn't have a response to that, so I kept walking out as people began giving me music requests to sing that night with the mystery Elder.

I never did find out who that Elder was. After about three nights we got in trouble and the singing ended. Besides this being probably the most romantic thing that has ever happened to me in my life, it also showed me that I do in fact, like my voice and that I do believe I am talented. This was huge in boosting my self-confidence in singing. It didn't matter how many people had told me they liked my voice; until I believed it myself, I wasn't confident. With that belief, I accepted and chose to see myself as a singer: not as the character on the stage, but the actual me. Because of that self-belief, I was able to come home from my mission and perform with confidence. I have had many opportunities to sing solos throughout the country. It all started with a little self-belief and self-acceptance.

How To Know When You Are Authentic

You are at peace

If you feel at peace in your life, you are likely living an authentic life. This doesn't mean life is always smooth sailing, but overall you have a peace that you are on the right track in your life. For me, it can be frustrating when people ask about why I'm not married and tell me to go on more dates. However, I have seen that when I am trying to force myself to go on a bunch of dates, I do not feel at peace. The peace for me comes when I try to be still and trust the Lord's timing like He has told me to. I feel I am living the life God wants for me, and that feels like the true path for me.

You don't have to prove yourself

The first draft of this book was almost double the size it is today. I wrote the majority of it years before I actually got serious about publishing. When I finally met with my editing team for the first time, before they even got started reading, they told me it was too long. As I read back over it to decide what to cut before giving it to them, I realized that almost a third of the book was a lot of me trying to show off, and prove how great I am. At the time I wrote it I didn't think I was enough, so I was trying to write a book to prove I was. As years passed and I grew to know and love myself more, I didn't feel like I needed to do that anymore. Instead, I really got clear on my desire to write this book to help women, and not to prove something to the world. It was then that this book really came together and it was easy to know what to cut and what to change and keep.

You like yourself

The easiest way to know if you are being authentic with your life is if you like yourself. It may seem strange that when you like yourself, you are being a genuine person. But what it means is that you are living in congruence with who you are. That doesn't mean you stop trying to grow or change. It just means you are very likely to be currently pursuing your passions and living in a way that is authentic to you. Authentic people tend to not care what others think of them. They are generally only concerned about what they think about themselves, and what God thinks of them.

It is easy to be kind

If you find that it is easy to be kind to others and happy for them even if they are more "successful" than you in anything, you are likely living your life in a way that is sincere. Jealousy is a pretty good sign that you are out of alignment with yourself. If I see someone doing something that makes me jealous, I try and think: am I willing to do what they did to get there? Would that really make me happy? If the answer is yes, I should start doing those things because that will probably help me get to know myself better and help me live authentically. I might even reach out to the person for advice. If the answer is no, I have no reason to be jealous because the things I have chosen to do with my life are more in line with who I really am and who I want to be.

If you struggle to be kind to people that you perceive to be inferior to you in some way, that is a quick way to know you are not being true to yourself. If you understood your true worth, you would recognize that worth in others and so would have no reason to be unkind. Authentic people tend to be the kindest people.

Turn To The Lord

More than anything else, it is important to grow your relationship with God. He knows you better than you know yourself. You spent an eternity with Him before you came to this earth. The closer you get to Him, the closer you will get to knowing your true self. He will help you on the journey of self-discovery as you let Him be a part of it. He might not give you a big sign that says "go to France!" or "study nursing!" but He will allow you to go through experiences that will teach you about you. They might be very hard experiences, because those often help us learn about who we really are deep down. As you seek Him in these moments, I know He will consecrate everything you go through for your learning and growth. Sometimes it takes years, but He will always show you why things happened the way they did. You might stand back one day in total awe at what He has helped you discover if you will but trust in Him and His timing.

The Authentic You

Samantha R.'s Story

"Well, it's a good thing you're pretty."

I loved music, I loved studying and schoolwork, and I loved random things like movies about little hobbits going on adventures. Yet, despite the joy that these things brought me, confused stares and awkward responses followed me throughout high school as people got to know me. I didn't play sports, I didn't know current music or movies, and I was involved in clubs and groups that I had a passion for, but that many didn't understand. It was all okay though because, as people would remind me,

> "it's a good thing you're pretty."

Was that all I was? As experience after experience with boys ended poorly, these words continued to echo in my head: "It's a good thing you're pretty. It's a good thing you're pretty. It's a good thing you're pretty." Slowly, I began to believe that every ended relationship, every negative experience, must've been because I was too weird or too different. The problem was definitely me because all I had going for me was that I was "pretty". Though I found joy in the interests I held, they always seemed like some sort of caveat to my character rather than a unique addition to who I was. In my second semester of college for instance, I distinctly remember standing on the shuttle bus, when I noticed a guy sitting two chairs away who was casting quick glances my way. Before I even had a moment to register what was happening, however, my mind instantly thought the words, "Yeah, he might think you're cute, but wait until he actually gets to know you. Then he won't be interested anymore".

As I left on my mission, I found myself reflecting on this experience many times. Though I taught many people about God's love and our eternal identity as children of God, I realized I didn't necessarily understand what that meant for me. I didn't know how to be who He wanted me to be because I wasn't always proud of who I was. How could I ever allow someone to love me when I didn't even love myself? How could I ever find a proper relationship when I was always so stressed that I would say or do something to mess it up-simply by being myself?

Like Nephi in the Book of Mormon, for those 18 months I felt that I was in my own wilderness. I felt my largest insecurities arise and my deepest problems surface. Yet, through hardship and trial, I began to learn about the nature of God. I learned more about Jesus Christ and His Infinite Atonement; I learned about His attributes and qualities. I began to understand things like faith, grace, temperance, hope, and charity through His life. As I did, I slowly began to learn more about myself as well. I began to question less which "box" I needed to fit *into*, and rather how I could more fully come *unto* the Savior. I learned that, like the Savior, I can be as quiet and as good at listening as He was while comforting Mary and Martha, while also being as energetic and happy as He was with the children. I can be fun and enjoyable to talk to like He was on the road to Emmaus, while also being as focused and spiritual as he was when giving the Intercessory prayer. Though there are many things I still love and enjoy *doing* every day, by coming to know the Savior my life was forever changed as I realized how freeing it is to instead focus on *becoming* more like the Savior.

Though I returned from my mission with a new and budding sense of self-worth and self-esteem, I have still struggled at times with the thought, "am I somehow going to mess all of this up? Is it all on my shoulders to find, meet, and marry the right person?" Whenever I become stressed or overwhelmed, however, my thoughts turn to Matthew 8:1-3.

1 When he was come down from the mountain, great multitudes followed him.

2 And, behold, there came a leper and worshipped him, saying, Lord, if thou wilt, thou canst make me clean.

3 And Jesus put forth his hand, and touched him, saying, I will; be thou clean. And immediately his leprosy was cleansed.

    Though we may not be dealing with a harrowing disease like leprosy, I have found myself on my knees many times, humbly pleading before the Lord for the deepest desires of my heart. I have prayed for relief from pain and pleaded for comfort in the aftermath of a relationship gone wrong. I have pleaded with the Lord countless times for guidance when dealing with emotions that have seemed too confusing to understand. I have prayed for happiness and peace amidst the stress of dating. Just like how we hope the Savior will answer the desires of our hearts, I am sure this leper feels the same. That is why it is such a wonderful moment when we read the words, "immediately his leprosy was cleansed". His righteous desire was fulfilled, and we pray for the same response to our own prayers. Before He heals the leper, however, it says that "Jesus put forth his hand, *and touched him*". Living in a time when leprosy was not only seen as a debilitating sickness, but also a sign of direct condemnation from God, lepers were humiliatingly ostracized and avoided in society. For a man to be desperate enough to go to an unknown Rabbi for healing-for that was who the Savior was at the time- shows a frantic search for relief that may hint to just how long this man must have been dealing with this disease. Though he *wanted* to be healed, one of His greatest *needs* at the time was to feel loved-to feel included and recognized for more than just his disease. In the moment that the Savior touched him, as a leper and not a healed man quite yet, the Savior addressed that need.

    Just like the leper in this story, the Lord knows the wants that we pray for. He hears every prayer and every outward expression of faith we utter, and he will answer our righteous desires in His own due time. Yet, I am grateful for a Savior who, just as he did by touching the leper, addresses our needs before addressing our wants. He knows the things we don't share, the pains that rest deep within our hearts, and through His Atoning sacrifice He wants to heal them and help us become who He sees us becoming.

So, though I don't know what my future holds, I know that the Lord will bless me with what I need. I know that He has divinely and uniquely created each one of us and that, as we come to know of Him, we will more fully and purely learn of ourselves. It is freeing and humbling to place my future in His hands-in the hands of the Healer who knows what I want, and more importantly what I need.

Chapter 3
Self-Love

"With the help of the scriptures, words of the prophets, and personal revelation, we gradually come to an awareness of our true nature and destiny. Once we grasp this reality, we can obtain the faith to move forward and overcome any obstacle standing in our way... including the obstacle of feelings of low self-worth." – Elder Glenn L Pace of the Seventy, *Confidence and Self-Worth*

Learning To Love Me

The first time I really remember trying to love myself was during my junior year of college. I was a theater major. This meant that your talents and abilities were important, but so was your physique. This is not necessarily in a bad way- but your body shape and your look do impact the kind of roles you are cast in for better or for worse.

This became a stumbling block for me. In high school it wasn't an issue because there wasn't too much competition. I was able to get the parts I wanted most of the time. But in college, looks did matter. We were told what our 'type' was based upon our looks. I believe the beauty of art is that you can break these boundaries. Shakespeare did it in his day- women couldn't be actors so men played the female roles. It is healthy to accept and be comfortable with who you are, so you can then make changes.

This was hard for me at the time though. I wanted to play whatever roles appealed to me, regardless of my look. It was not that I always wanted to be the lead, but that I hated the idea of limitations. And in my mind, my weight was a major thing holding me back. I wasn't small enough to be the lead roles, and not big enough to be the funny characters or villains.

I was already struggling with body issues and some levels of anxiety and self-confidence. One night during my junior year, I was so overwhelmed I didn't want to deal with it anymore! I wanted a change. After all my roommates were in bed and I was alone in my room, I turned off the lights and stood in the middle of the room. I then started whispering things I wished were true about myself. "I'm beautiful". "I'm talented". I cried but I kept pushing through. I kept repeating things that I wanted to be true until finally, probably after about an hour, I started to believe these things just a little bit. Then I allowed myself to go to bed.

Let Weak Things Become Strong

Sometimes talking about self-love can feel like talking about becoming prideful. We know we must show dependence on the Lord, and that we have been given weaknesses (Ether 12:27). However, the same scripture that talks about us having weaknesses also says that God makes these weak things become strong. There's an old talk that I love that says:

> "Too often we wallow in our weaknesses so much that we do not allow 'weak things' to 'become strong.' Our condition is frequently misdiagnosed as humility, when in reality it is a lack of confidence." – Elder Glenn L Pace of the Seventy
> *Confidence and Self-Worth*

The Lord doesn't want us spending all of our time thinking about our inabilities or weaknesses. One way we can show our trust and faith in Him is to recognize strengths that He is creating in us. That is what self-love is. It is recognizing that as a daughter of God, you are a wonderful being, full of divine potential and able to do much good in the world.

Self-love for me has been a journey since that night in my room in college. I truly believe if women loved themselves

Self-Love

correctly, many of society's issues would go away. There would be less tolerance of bad relationships, less inequality, and more love in the world. If you love yourself as you deserve, you will make the world a better place.

Self-love begins with a desire for change, and lots of trial and error and practice. This chapter is devoted to ideas and thoughts to help you on your journey of self-worth, but there are many other ways to grow it as well. As you turn to the Lord and seek His guidance, you will be able to more fully develop the confidence you desire.

Perfection

Wanting to be perfect before being happy is a barrier to self-acceptance. This is true regardless of your relationship status, but there is a bit of this that is specific to singles. If you're always thinking, 'I just need to change and then I'll get married', then you might beat yourself up when marriage doesn't come around. If you cannot see yourself as whole or awesome as a single person all on your own, you might be in for a difficult time whether single or not.

I struggled with perfection when I was learning Spanish on my mission. I thought a good motivator for myself would be to not be satisfied or happy with my progress learning the language until I spoke Spanish perfectly. Instead, this just made me super stressed about the language, and probably set me behind the average missionary learning Spanish by a couple of months. This is what happens when we focus too much on the end result, and don't take joy in the journey. I couldn't appreciate the miracle of learning a second language, because I was too busy being upset about not being perfect. It wasn't until I got my second companion, six months into my mission that this started to change. She was a gringa like me, so Spanish was not a native language to her. She had been out much longer than I had, and yet her Spanish was not perfect! "Oh no!", I thought at first. Seeing the less-than-perfect language skills of my companion who had been out longer than me made me worry that more time and practice with the language would still not allow me to achieve my goal. How could I be happy if I wasn't perfect at Spanish nine months in?!

But as I started to observe her, I saw that she was an amazing missionary! She was enthusiastic, and people were opening up their doors to us a lot more than I had ever seen previously. We were finding so many people to teach, and so many people were listening to us- even though we didn't speak Spanish very well! I started to realize that the gift of tongues did not mean that I would suddenly speak beautiful Spanish, which is what I had thought would happen. That never happened once throughout my whole mission. Instead, the gift of tongues for me was doing the best I could and letting the spirit touch a person's heart and allow them to hear what they needed. My speaking ability didn't magically change. They were hearing the spirit- not the words coming out of my mouth. My desire to be perfect and my lack of gratitude for the blessings I had were getting in the way of miracles happening. When I finally got over needing to speak perfectly and was able to appreciate the amazing experience I was having, I was able to relax and start having fun.

I never became perfect at speaking Spanish, even after a full 18 months out. But I understood and spoke enough to be able to do what the Lord asked me to do. Perfection and ingratitude can really get in the way of happiness. In my experience, the more we learn to let things go and be grateful for what we have right now, the happier we will be.

Ideas To Grow Your Self-Worth

Speak Positive Affirmations

Speak positive affirmations to yourself morning and night to really get the ball rolling and practice self-love. I have a mentor who is a multi-millionaire and who is *amazing* at consistently doing affirmations. Once I asked him what to do if I just don't believe the affirmations about myself or that I can accomplish the goals that I want. He said that when he was first starting to do affirmations, he felt the same way. He started saying his goals and affirmations, but one night it was just too much. He felt *so* worthless. He crumpled up the paper he had them written on and threw it away. But during the night he couldn't stop thinking about it. He was desperate for a life change. He got out of bed, pulled the paper out of the trash, straightened it out, and read the affirmations again. He hasn't stopped doing that since, and is now extremely successful spiritually, mentally, and careerwise. Read until you believe.

This idea of saying or reading things as if they have already happened is a pattern in the scriptures. Isaiah is the king of affirmations! He wrote consistently about Christ as if the events had already happened. For example, when Abinadi is quoting Isaiah's words about Jesus in chapter 14 of the Book of Mormon, it says: "...he *was* wounded for our transgressions, he *was* bruised for our iniquities…" (verse 5, emphasis added) Even though Abinadi lived hundreds of years before Christ would come, and Isaiah even longer before that, they spoke as if it had already happened! Affirmations are something prophets have used, and we can too in our small way.

Take Care of Yourself

Our physical bodies often impact our self-love. Everyone I know goes through some form of body image issues, no matter what size they are or how perfect they might seem to other people.

What if I told you I could give you the perfect body, but then you only got to live one more day, and then your life was over? You'd refuse, right? That's because having life is a greater gift than having a perfect body.

Little by little, line upon line, year by year, I've been able to improve my self-image. It has taken time and positive self-talk. Most importantly, I made the choice to believe that I am a healthy and beautiful person *right now*. Because of this, my brain and body help me to make choices that support these beliefs. My body is my friend rather than my enemy. I am grateful for my body and see it as a gift. I tell my body I love it, and that's why I take care of it. I'm taking the time to try and listen to my body and get to know it. Exercising is easier, and so is eating healthier - because I decided I am a healthy person, and that is what healthy people do. Rather than being discouraged with how long it takes, I love myself right now. I tell myself how proud I am of the changes that have been made, and I look forward to a long and healthy life.

Everyone's journey to love their physical body is different. I want to encourage you to start loving your body right where it is today if you're not already doing so.

Find your inner Cinderella

I have learned that for me, being able to cook well builds a lot of self-confidence and self-love. I started cooking about four dinners a week when I became a foster mom. One night, my daughter decided to stay out late with her older sister, so she wouldn't be eating dinner with me. I had planned on making enchilada soup, but I started to think it wasn't worth making it just for myself. Then I remembered an episode of *Queer Eye* where Antoni talks about how making food is a way to show love to yourself. I decided to make the soup and it was actually a great experience! I made it just for me, because I am worth it, and I felt good because of that.

For other people, *not* cooking might be a form of self-love. Everyone's situation is different, and you might need different things at different times. Just keep getting to know yourself and it will get easier to know how to love yourself.

Another skill you can learn to increase self-love is cleaning. Putting in the effort to do work like cleaning releases happy endorphins. It's hard to believe it before taking action, but cleaning can really help when you struggle with depression. When I start praying to God for help because I'm depressed, He often tells me to get up and do something. For me, cleaning is the most obvious and easy thing to do right then and there. Sometimes I really feel like I can't. But if I can get myself to set a three-minute timer, and just start doing it, I find that my mood lifts and I am able to go longer than my timer. The key is to just get started. If I look at Facebook when I am depressed, I don't feel any better. If I clean something even for just three minutes, I do feel better. I also feel like I can respect myself better when I take care of my living space, and that increases my self-worth.

However, please remember that even self-love needs to be unconditional. If you're depressed or in another situation where you can't do the things you think you should, you *still* deserve love.

Love your Look

One of the most important conversations I have had about self-love was with one of my sisters. At the time, she was a senior in high school and I had recently returned from my mission. I was trying to decide if I finally wanted to give up my flat iron and embrace my curly hair. My younger sister had already embraced hers. One day I said to her: "Do people just love your hair?" She said, "I don't know, but I do!" This changed my whole perspective. So much of what I did with my looks, and my style, had to do with what I thought other people would like- I had never really thought about what I liked or wanted.

Some girls know their look really well and love it. Growing up I wanted to look cute and have good style, but I never actually put time into it. Instead, I would just envy others who looked great and wish I could be more like that. The same thing applied to makeup. While growing up, I was not at all interested in wearing makeup, but I always thought in the back of my mind that I wanted to wear makeup when I grew up.

As I got through college, I just kept thinking that I wasn't old enough to really dress up, and wear makeup yet. I had to have a big career or be married or… It finally clicked one day that I was ready if I wanted to be!

Know Thyself

I started buying cute clothes I actually liked and wanted. I bought clothes that made me feel comfortable with the job I was falling in love with. It was a process, because at first I just copied the styles of my friends. Eventually, I had to rely on my own opinion and not worry so much about being different and enjoy being myself.

Next, I asked friends to teach me about makeup. It was way out of my element at first, but after just a few weeks I started to become comfortable with it. YouTube is also a great resource for makeup tips. I think part of the reason I wasn't getting into makeup and clothes is that I was worried that a boy might like me for my looks instead of who I am. But as I've embraced being who I want to be, I've accepted that some boys like girls with makeup and some don't, and that's okay! Some people might see makeup as fake but I like it, and my opinion of myself is the only one that matters (besides God). As for boys: I just want one man who is in love with the real, authentic me- and that me happens to really like makeup and heels.

As I have become more comfortable with clothes, hair, and makeup, I feel great! I feel confident. I love myself more, because I feel like I'm taking care of myself better. Some days I'm in my office alone all day, and I don't see anyone except my roommates in the evening. But I still dress up because I like it. I have become more of who I always wanted to be. I chose to stop waiting to *someday* be my ideal woman, and I'm working on being her now. I feel better at work, I feel better in public and enjoy taking pictures.

Maybe you already dress really well and have great style. But maybe you want to try something new and are nervous. Go for it! Try a new lipstick. Wear a new style of shoes. If it ends up not being a good fit and you don't like it, you've learned something! A tip to help you get started is to go through your closet and throw out everything you don't like or don't wear or don't want any more. Then you will *have* to buy new things. That helped me because after

I got rid of all the things I didn't like, I ran out of clothes to wear pretty fast.

Create Good Habits

Something else that can improve self-confidence is creating habits. Good habits have the power to totally change your life. I learned this by studying two books - *The Compound Theory* and *The Geometry of Success*. All the successful people I know are really good at consistently doing little things on a daily basis. God knows this better than anyone. That's why He is constantly inviting us to have daily prayer and scripture study. The little habits we create will bring us joy and back to His presence. They will also give us meaningful and fulfilling lives now and help us face our challenges. Sometimes it can seem hard or pointless to focus on little things but added up over years you can see the difference. Sometimes I hear girls say they wish they knew the scriptures better. It's not too late! If you study a little bit each day, you will know them. It just takes time.

If you have bad habits that you want to break, here are some tips. Think about *where* they happen. Can you find any patterns? If so, consider making some changes. If you struggle to do your homework when you are on your bed, try doing it somewhere else. If you struggle with bad thoughts, notice where you are when this happens. Can you change your situation? Can you go somewhere else? At the very least, once you are aware you can consciously prep yourself so that next time you are in that place, you know to put up your defenses against those bad habits.

You might also try replacing the bad habit with something else. Do you bite your nails? Try chewing gum. You can also do something to help you remember, like dipping your fingers in cayenne pepper! That's a quick way to tell your brain not to subconsciously bite your nails anymore.

Know Thyself

Push Yourself

Taking risks can also increase your self-love, because it might help you see what you are capable of and grow your skills and abilities. Sheri Dew often shares her biggest regret at firesides/talks, etc. Sheri Dew was 5'10" by the time she was 11 years old! She loves basketball and played it well, all through high school. When she was in college, she really wanted to join the basketball team. She went all the way to the gym where tryouts were, but never got the courage to go in. Years later Sister Dew was asked to speak at an event by BYU athletic director Elaine Michaelis, who was the coach the year Sister Dew would have tried out. She shared her regret at not trying out for the team during that event. Afterwards, Elaine came up to her and told her that she remembered that year well because they were one player short. They never found someone to be the tall center. ("Sheri Dew: Living the Unexpected Life", by Doug Robinson, *Deseret News*, Oct 2002.)

I love what Sister Dew says as her take-away from this experience: "The truth is, no one can take your place". But she also says she still hasn't gotten over it. For me, the "if only" feeling is one of the worst! That's why I think it's important to take risks. It's scary to go beyond your limits and try new things, but it helps you live a life without regret and can lead you down amazing paths. You can have opportunities you wouldn't otherwise have, and what better time to do it than when you are single?

Learning to be open to things that take you out of your comfort zone can help you grow in unexpected ways and give you amazing opportunities. When I got back from my mission, people started asking me if they could set me up with people. The idea terrified me, and I said "no". My friend and I were at a wedding and my friend wanted me to go with her to see if some boys at another table wanted to dance. Again, I said "no". I never wanted to do anything that took me out of my comfort zone. With time I started to realize that by saying no to everything new or different, I was not becoming who I wanted to become, or having more dating opportunities like I wanted. It's ok if things make you nervous and uncomfortable sometimes, but growth comes when you push yourself. I eventually decided that I would be the kind of person who was open to new opportunities. It didn't happen overnight, but I feel like I have improved over the years and I love what I have been able to do and accomplish because of that. Risk taking is kind of like faith building. You take a step in the dark and have to trust that things will work out. Risk taking can bring lots of fulfillment and fun to your life. And the best part is if things don't work out, you are still better for it because you learned something about yourself you might never have otherwise.

This is not the same thing as saying yes to everything that someone asks you to do. A lot of women have a hard time saying no to things and then taking on too much. It's about being willing to try new things, not about putting more on your plate than you can handle.

Travel

Take this time to travel! Travel is probably the number one thing people regret not doing more of while single. Traveling can be overwhelming or scary if you haven't traveled much before. But it is always a learning and growing experience, and (usually) very relaxing and stress relieving! It's also a skill that is helpful in being a better mom, because then you will be able to take your family on trips without so much frustration and stress. Going on family vacations is bonding time, and great for kids to grow and learn and experience the world. So treat yourself now to little vacations. Don't let yourself get comfortable sitting around at home. Travel far and wide. Do it through a humanitarian group! One thing I have learned from my many travels is that I enjoy it more when I am serving- either the people that come with me on the trip, or people at the place I am visiting. There are some really cheap trips available this way. Before one of my sisters left for her mission, the two of us went to Mexico to help at an orphanage. We went with the organization: A Child's Hope Foundation. It was a fabulous five-day trip where we got to serve and have fun *and* it was super cheap!

If traveling to a faraway place seems scary, then here's some advice. Don't leave the country on your first trip; start by leaving the state. If you have a friend or someone in your ward who is good at traveling, plan a trip with them. They will help you know what to plan for, and what to get ready. If you are new to flying, having a friend with you who is familiar with airports will build your confidence a lot. Learning how to easily get in and out of an airport and understanding all the signs are important skills on their own. It will build your travel confidence so you can expand to farther and farther destinations, and even be able to go alone if you want to.

Would you like to stay in a foreign place a little longer? You can look for temporary jobs at your chosen destination. Some countries actually let you work and live at an Airbnb or hostel for a month or so. You can run the front desk for a couple of hours- speaking English is a valuable skill in the travel industry- and in exchange you get a room for free.

But why is traveling so great, and what does it have to do with self-love? Travel helps you understand the world and yourself better. It also gives your life beauty and adventure. Traveling brings you into the present- it's hard to think about the past or future too much when you are in such a new environment, doing things totally different from your norm. Your spirit needs this sometimes. You leave your everyday world temporarily and it changes you for the better. You can be whoever you want to be when you are on vacation. You can leave behind your labels and cares and just be. Moving to a new place can also be helpful for letting go and leaving behind old things. But on a vacation, it's more freeing because it is not permanent. During this time of singleness, you can more easily do this too, because you don't have a family dependent on you to be a certain way.

Another great thing about traveling is you learn about other cultures, and you can apply what you learn to your life to make it better. I went to Amsterdam one year, and my world changed. Bikes were everywhere! There were more places to park a bike than a car! Everyone was biking. And not just for recreation- business people were going to work on their bikes. We asked someone, "What if you have an important meeting? You don't want to show up all sweaty, right?" "No one cares," the person answered. We were amazed! My friend and I went on a bike tour and nearly died- people drive their bikes super fast and there are just so many of them! Coming home, it really made me want to bike to work. But I was worried about how long it would take. I looked it up on Google maps. It took 17 minutes- just 17 minutes to bike to work when it takes me 10 minutes to drive. I couldn't believe it, so I decided to give it a try. I worried about problems I might have, but I decided to just do it. I grabbed my roommate's bike one morning, and away I went. I made it just fine. I was slightly self-conscious, but when I remembered how European it is to bike, my confidence rose. It was awesome! I saved on gas and mileage on my car every day, got in exercise by doing something that I needed to do anyway (get to work) and only added 14 minutes to my day. I never would have thought to try this without traveling.

Let Dreams Grow with You

Sometimes -not all the time- giving up *is* the right thing to do. Self-love can mean allowing your dreams to change and evolve when you do. Maybe you've had a childhood dream that you wanted badly and told everyone about, but as you get older that dream doesn't have the same spark it used to. However, you feel like you can't back down, because then you would be giving up.

It is okay to change. I have always loved the story of Peter Pan. My mom called me Wendy when I was young because I never wanted to grow up. I cried on my eighth birthday because I thought I was so old. I remember the first time I learned that Wendy did grow up. I was heartbroken. But as I have grown up, I have changed. I always wanted to be an actress, even if the world was against me! I participated in theater all through high school and went on to get my bachelor's degree in Musical Theater.

Every time I didn't get cast in something in college, I would just work harder. I was determined to be the best. Eventually, I did become very good. I made it into the elite program at my university and had some great opportunities and performances. But during my mission and last year at the university, I slowly came to find that there were things I wanted to do more than perform.

It was hard to let go of that dream. I had found strength of character as I fought against the odds of being a short chubby girl but still contending for the lead roles! However, I came to find that other things gave me just as much if not more fulfillment.

It was interesting that the hardest part of changing for me was worrying about what other people would think about me. I was embarrassed that my choice might be seen as giving up or backing down. Everyone knew me as the actress- it was a big part of my identity. In my high school I was Speech and Drama Sterling Scholar, and my Senior year I was voted, "most likely to succeed".

Finally, at the end of my senior year in college, I decided to let it all go- put that life in the past, and start fresh. I didn't know what I wanted to do right then, but I knew it wasn't theater. It took a leap of faith. Years later I can honestly say I have never regretted my decision to leave theater. I probably would never have written this book if I hadn't left that behind, or done a number of other things I have done. Letting go- giving up on that dream- has not been sad. It was a stepping stone in helping me blossom into the person I am, and I like what I have become. I love what I am doing in the world. I don't want to go back.

Give yourself permission to give up sometimes! We are creators. It's okay for us to create new paths and dreams. Those four years I spent in the University studying theater were not a waste. I developed talents and skills and made some fabulous and life-changing friendships. I also drew closer to God during that time. I learned to start loving myself. I am grateful for all of those things. Sometimes we've got to go down a side trail for a while to learn things that will help us on the longer path of our life. Life in the end is about getting to the Celestial Kingdom, not finding the perfect career, or completing every dream. Anything helping you towards the path of reaching your potential and becoming more like God is doing the right thing.

The Results

As you develop self-worth, your life will improve in ways you may not even expect. I have seen this in my life, and most especially with dating. I had an experience once with a guy that I liked. We were talking, and he gave me his opinion about something in a way that made me feel my opinion was stupid. When I was younger, I would have assumed that he was correct and I wouldn't have confronted him. But, because I had learned to value myself more, I didn't back down.

I simply said, "Did my opinion offend you?"
He said, "No."
I responded, "Well I do not deserve to be talked to that way."

And then the craziest thing happened. He apologized! And asked me how he could make it up to me. I was totally not expecting that. Not only did I feel validated, but I felt cared for by him. It was a double win. Your life changes depending on how you see yourself.

Self-love is such an important thing to learn, regardless of your relationship status. It will make us better in whatever roles we have in life. I believe it's truly one of the most important things we can do to make the world a better place. If we really understand our divine worth, we will have the confidence to stand up for goodness and serve those around us. Self-love is beautiful and so needed in this world of fear and hate. You can change yourself and the world by loving yourself a little more every day!

Know Thyself

Amy L.'s Story

I'm 28 years old and I'd say I'm a catch!

One of the hard parts about being from Utah is that there are so many options, for the guys and for the girls. Commitment anxiety is a thing, how do you know if they're the "one" that you're going to spend eternity with? That's a lot to ask for someone our age, and a lot of times the Lord doesn't necessarily give super strong revelation on if it's a yes or a no, because it's a choice that we get to choose every day.

Ever since I got back from my mission I "officially dated" probably 15 guys, but they only lasted for about a month. Until recently I've been the one breaking up with them. I felt like I knew what I wanted and so if I didn't see any progression towards marriage, then what was the point in continuing a romantic relationship?

I believe that we are created to need people, and naturally it feels like we should just need one person to fill all our needs. This isn't the case in or outside of marriage. While we are designed to thrive in a partnership relationship, God didn't design us to only be fulfilled by it and condemn all those who don't have it. Even in marriage I have heard many people saying that they have found other people to fill needs that their husband can't - whether that's with the Lord, friends or family or personal achievement and growth, we have a lot of needs that can be filled in many ways.

Take it from me--I'm a very needy person and I'm realizing that I'm more needy than I originally thought -- I have a *lot* of needs!

One of my challenges with dating is trusting a man to fill those needs--especially if I'm writing them off quickly as someone that doesn't have eternal potential. It is vulnerable to let someone love you, especially someone of the opposite gender who is wired to think differently than you. I think much of my life I have been avoiding letting men love me because that means I'd have to learn

Self-Love

how to communicate with them and open myself up to the possibility of pain. With girls--especially roommates it's been easy to let them in quickly because they're safe! I'm not going to marry them or commit eternity to them, and yet they get me and know me and love me! I can be vulnerable with them. What's been interesting is that in some cases I've let them in so much and then expected them to handle all of me and all of my needs which just isn't feasible for anyone, especially just a roommate or friend! I have actually lost some really close friends because I didn't know how to put proper boundaries around my needs.

    Another thing I've learned is that self-love is extremely important! I've been thinking that a guy will love or care about me once I'm more or less "_____". I then subconsciously have put that on myself that I'll love myself once I'm more or less "_____". The ironic thing is that I then wonder why men don't love me. If I don't love myself, then how can I expect to receive love or believe someone else would love me that much? This went on to the point where I wouldn't even accept love from God. I'd almost just think "yeah, I know that He loves me, He loves everyone, but I need to do _____ or be more _____ to really deserve his love". It was a black and toxic hole. When anyone showed me real love, because I didn't believe I was loveable, I would cling to that because I had been starving myself and refusing to love myself. Crazy! I wasn't making a conscious effort to identify the negative thought patterns I'd had about myself and to realize that if someone else didn't love or care about me, that was no reflection of my worth or who I was. Just because someone's preference is for apples doesn't mean that the most delectable and delicious peach loses any worth.

    I also think as female Christians we think that we need to think of others more than ourselves. The second great commandment says to love others *as* ourselves. The best form of self-love is positive self-talk and having your own back -- meaning that if anything were to hurt or not serve you, you destroy that thing! Many times, our own negative thoughts can be extremely harmful, so loving ourselves means we cannot tolerate that kind of thinking. If you're feeling sad about a situation know that your thoughts determine your feelings, every time. Is that thought serving you as a queen and daughter of God?

Section 2
Moving Forward

"Ye cannot behold with your natural eyes, for the present time, the design of your God concerning those things which shall come hereafter, and the glory which shall follow after much tribulation" (D&C 58:2-3)

Chapter 4
Expectations

"Life is like an old time rail journey- delays, sidetracks, smoke, dust, cinders, and jolts, interspersed only occasionally by beautiful vistas and thrilling bursts of speed. The trick is to thank the Lord for letting you have the ride." - President Gordon B. Hinckley, *Ensign*, Nov. 1984:86 (Jenkin Loyd Jones, a columnist)

Unmet Expectations

I remember looking in the mirror one day around age 26 and really seeing my wrinkles for the first time. Initially, I wasn't sure what to think - I hadn't thought much at all about aging. But then I thought: I don't want to have wrinkles on my wedding day. That stung. I didn't expect to get wrinkles until after having kids! Don't you get married when you look your prettiest, and then you can start going downhill? And here I was, watching my prime slip away, without a marriage prospect in sight. I needed to get married quickly, if only to preserve my prettiest self for those marriage photos that will be my most-looked-at photos by me and my future kids.

I hadn't even realized I had the expectation to get married when my skin and hair were still youthful looking, until I saw that it was starting to slip away.

When expectations go unmet, there is frustration, sorrow, and depression. Proverbs 13:12 says "Hope deferred maketh the heart sick: but when the desire cometh, it is a tree of life." I believe that is an accurate description of what it feels like to want to get married, but feel like you are powerless to make it happen, and not have that expectation met. Your heart is sick.

But that kind of despondent thinking never gets the results I want. So, how do we deal with these unmet expectations? How do we deal with sick hearts?

Managing Personal Expectations

Keep it in Perspective

When I am frustrated about being single, I remember that just because I have been single and there is no end in sight, I am not the only person having to deal with unmet expectations. There are people who are divorced, or that really want to have kids and can't, as well as people with illnesses that place limitations on their lives. Maybe they had goals and dreams to change the world, but now they can't even get out of bed. Singleness isn't the only trial of unmet expectations that creates heart ache. Sometimes I hear single people complain about how singles wards shouldn't exist. But I also hear about couples with infertility who go to church and see all the children and get so depressed they stop going to church. It might be a blessing that we don't have to see all the happy families every Sunday.

Sometimes it is easy to think you are the only one experiencing heartache. Satan is the master isolator. If he can get us to think we are all alone, we don't get help and we stay in the pain. That devil on your shoulder is trying to keep you thinking you're the only one with issues.

I'm not even just talking about the fact that 51% of women over the age of 18 are single in the church. I'm also talking about other life situations.

Recently in a Relief Society class, one sister talked about how she wanted to serve a mission. She knew that it might not happen, because she was born with a health condition. However, she went ahead and started working on her papers. Her doctor said she should be able to go. Her bishop gave his approval, and the stake president as well. However a month after her papers were in at church headquarters, the answer came back that no, she couldn't go.

When she got this news, she was heartbroken. She had righteous desires- why was she being denied the opportunity to do a lot of good in the world? Was she not good enough to do it? She felt worth *less* because everyone else around her was serving. She talked about going to BYU and how there didn't seem to be a single person her age on campus, because they were all on missions. She'd never be able to change her health condition- she felt she had been born broken and not as valuable as everyone else around her.

This is what a lot of single people feel like, as well as people that can't have kids, or get divorced, or lose a spouse. We actually all have pretty similar experiences, just in different ways. The emotions are similar. There is much in common in the human experience.

When I hear about other people struggling, it definitely helps me remember to stop getting so wrapped up in my own problems. I try and remember that even if I was married, life wouldn't be all rosy and rainbows. There are difficulties in marriage just as hard as being single. Divorce, death, infertility, health struggles for you or a spouse, wayward children... there's a huge list of challenges and singleness is only one.

Faith in Christ, not in the Outcome

In that same relief society lesson, after hearing the sister's experience of not being able to serve a mission, another sister said that her dad was battling with cancer. She asked how could they keep moving forward? How did this sister who couldn't go on a mission keep moving forward? The mission sister shared how a big part of it was allowing herself to feel the grief. I too agree that this is important. Part of getting through and over things is allowing ourselves to feel our emotions, even when we talk to God. But I think there is something else important that goes along with any trial- especially as we see sometimes people are healed from sickness, sometimes they are not. Sometimes people get married, sometimes they do not. The way to get through it is to have faith in Jesus Christ, *not* in the results or outcomes we are hoping for. If my faith is in marriage, then if I don't get married by the time I think I am supposed to, I might fall away from the church. The same is true if my faith depends on the person being healed, or being able to go on a mission. But if our faith is in Jesus Christ, we can move forward despite the circumstances.

"But if not" Attitude

We can also choose to have what I call a "but if not" attitude. When my baby sister had cancer my first year in college, I had to learn this. My thought process was something like: "I desperately want my sister to be healed. *But if not*, I will still have faith and believe in Christ." This thought process helps me not put 'limits on my discipleship', as my dad calls it.

This idea of a "but if not" attitude came from an article I read in the *New Era* several years ago. It talked about how Abinadi in the Book of Mormon, and Shadrach, Meshach, and Abednego in the Bible, were in similar situations. Both Abinadi, and those three friends, were told they would be burnt to death unless they denied God. Both Abinadi and the three young men refused to do so. In Daniel 3, versus 17-18, the boys give their response to King Nebuchadnezzar when he says he is going to throw them into the furnace: "If it be so, our God whom we serve is able to deliver us from the burning fiery furnace, and he will deliver us out of thine hand, O king. *But if not*, be it known unto thee, O king, that we will not serve thy gods, nor worship the golden image which thou hast set up." (emphasis added) They had faith that God would deliver them. They also had faith that if it was their time to go, God would take them.
Their faith did not depend on the outcome of their situation.

Abinadi had equal faith. He had such powerful faith that when he was delivering his message from God to King Noah and the wicked priests, anyone who tried to touch him would be killed.

But after that speech, Abinadi was burnt to death by fire. This had nothing to do with how much God loved either party. He did not love Shadrach, Meshach, and Abednego more than He loved Abinadi. God has a plan and purpose for each person's life, both while on earth and afterwards too. He provides the way for us to accomplish our purposes.

I have needed to apply this concept to my life. Sometimes when I am sad about being single, I think: "I will get married! *But if not*, I will still serve my Master, Jesus Christ". Sometimes I really have to remind myself that marriage will happen! *But*, even if it never did, I would be faithful to the end. When Elder Bednar came to my mission, he asked the question, "does your faith depend on the results you think you will get?" When I'm feeling frustrated with God, I have found that it is usually because I was expecting a certain outcome in a situation. Elder Bednar's question helps me remember that real faith isn't based on the results I want. It's based on Jesus Christ.

The sister who couldn't serve a mission is not worth *less*. Neither is anyone else who doesn't receive the blessings they asked for in this life. We would do well to not define ourselves by the things we are not or don't have, and not judge others for those things either. When I was in my early twenties, I would look at sisters in their older twenties and sort of pity them or feel sorry for them. This kind of attitude isn't good for anyone. Most singles are incredible people- being incredible has *nothing* to do with getting married. Marriage is not a reward for being awesome.

In fact, what a terrible way to think about it! I hadn't really thought about it until I listened to a podcast called "All-In" hosted by Morgan Jones. In one of the episodes, she interviewed Mallory Everton, from the original cast of Studio C. This episode was all about being single in the church- and both Morgan and Mallory were 29-year-old single women at the time of the episode. I love their thoughts on being single. Mallory said something along the lines of: Getting a husband isn't a trophy, or blue ribbon. They are a person, and we are doing a disservice for ourselves and this other person when we treat marriage as a prize to be won. When we talk about 'graduating' from the singles ward, we are implying that work or something must have been done to achieve that graduation. This is simply hurting, not helping. So many women have this idea that once they fix something about themselves, or are ready, then they will get married. I also loved what Morgan said on this episode. She saw her younger 21-year-old sister get married. She noted that she herself was definitely more 'ready' for marriage than her little sister was. Being ready has zero to do with getting married. When we keep thinking about marriage this way, we are putting untrue thoughts in our minds about why people aren't married, and it creates a lot of anxiety in people who are single. It makes them think: I just have to find the one thing to fix! Or I just have to get ready! In reality none of this is true.

Judged by our hearts

Once when I was low during college, I remember thinking: If I never get married, will I still follow Jesus? I decided, Yes, I would. I didn't understand how important this commitment was until years later. I have seen women leave the church, and often it is linked to not being married by a certain time. I do not take lightly the moments I have been given to work on building my faith in Christ, rather than in desired outcomes. Faith must be in God, not what I want or expect.

When things don't go according to plan or expectations, it can be easy to blame God, or question His love. However, if we let them, these kinds of experiences can help us to do a gospel reset. We can check in with our testimonies, and make sure our faith is in God and Jesus Christ, and not in the results we expect.

I see this often in personal revelation. I will get an answer from God about something, and I will think it means one thing. When that thing doesn't happen, I think I must not really be hearing God. However, months or years down the road I will go back and read what I wrote down. I suddenly see that what I thought was going to happen was how I interpreted it- that I misunderstood or just tried to make things fit into my agenda. God knows what I need and want better than I do; I need to work more on seeing things His way instead of trying to fit His ways into my ways.

Something that brings me comfort is the knowledge that I will ultimately be judged for the desires of my heart, not all the external results of my life. (Alma 41:5) Of course I want to raise good children and have wonderful grandchildren as my legacy. Sometimes I get anxious at the idea of not having those things, or at least at not having a husband. Do people judge me for not being married? Do they think there is something wrong with me? Who knows. Maybe. One thing I have learned as an entrepreneur is that what other people think of me is none of my business. God is the judge I care most about, and He knows that if I was given the opportunity to marry a worthy man who was my equal and loved me back I would, and I would raise Him up an awesome family. God knows I am trying, and that's what is important to Him, whether or not I actually get the results I want or not.

Waiting on God

One time when I was at a Financial Seminar, I sat next to this lady who was super sweet. We began talking on a break, and I found out that she was a member of the church. She told me about how soon after she was married, she received a revelation that she would have kids. She was so excited! But years started passing, and no kids. She was frustrated and upset, especially with God. Finally, after six years of waiting, she had her first kid. She told me that she wished she hadn't wasted those six years! She could have done so much. She had had an idea for a business she wanted to start, but instead she focused on the frustration and sadness of not having kids. I was really inspired by her and decided that day that I didn't want to waste my waiting time. I know God allowed her to open up to me that day so that I could learn the importance of not wasting time given.

Expectations

    I think one of the reasons I have this "waiting time" is so that I can find a way to make money for my family. More and more, both moms and dads need to work because it can be hard to provide for a family with one income. I want to have something awesome figured out that I can do part time and from home but that makes some good money by the time I am married. That's probably not the only reason why I have this waiting time, but it is something that motivates me to try new things and work hard right now. And that makes me feel like I am not wasting my "waiting time".

    I wish I knew my timeline. Joseph in Egypt probably wished he knew the answer to how long he would be in prison. One of the most beloved prophets in the Bible was imprisoned for 15 years (during his prime dating years!). How easy it would be to feel abandoned by God in that situation.

    But Joseph didn't despair. He changed the lives of the people around him by teaching the gospel to the prisoners and guards. His relationship with God grew.

    I don't think Joseph was being a missionary because he thought it would get him out of jail more quickly. Single people do some of God's most important work, like Joseph spreading the gospel. This is an important work to the Lord. Do we use our singleness as an excuse not to serve, not to progress, not to become our best and most divine selves?

    Joseph was not in prison because he deserved it or God was punishing him. He was a good kid, and his brothers were jealous. That's how he ended up in that situation. Perhaps the Lord used the experience to teach Joseph. He learned patience and humility, and probably how to be happy and joyful no matter his circumstances. He later became a great ruler in Egypt. I'm sure he often thought back on his prison years. They were a really long part of his life. Perhaps the waiting in prison is what made Joseph into the great leader that he was. He certainly got good at seeking and receiving revelation with dreams during that time. God makes some of his best people wait. What a gift to be able to count ourselves part of that group!

We do not need to qualify for marriage by learning the right lessons during our "waiting time" of singleness. It doesn't work like that. But I do think there are things that are easier to learn while being single- time to grow and do things that would be harder while chasing a bunch of small children. There are many ways we can serve, too, if we are allowing ourselves to be instruments in God's hands during this time, and He certainly has work for us to do if we are open and willing.

I'm sure there were times when Joseph was tempted to say to God: "God, if I wasn't in prison I could be doing so much more good for you!" I feel like I say this a lot to God. "God, if I was married I could be making the world a better place by raising up righteous children and setting an example! Etc., etc." But even though it might seem true from our viewpoint, that there is more good that could be done, that isn't God's plan. What's stopping me from serving and helping others and being an example today, right where I am? Haven't I been given people to minister to? Don't I have neighbors and siblings and friends that could be blessed and helped by me? Why do I need to wait to be married with kids to be doing good in the world? This single time might feel a bit like a prison, but like Joseph I can use this time to bless others and prepare to be a great leader now and in the future for God.

When it's meant to be, it will be.

During a particularly trying time dealing with my singleness, I was frustrated and worried. I have learned that it is hard for me to get personal revelation when I am feeling those emotions. Because I knew that about myself, I was working on relaxing, accepting, and being grateful for what I do have.

On a Sunday as I was taking the sacrament, the spirit suddenly brought a song to my remembrance. This is a pretty common way for the spirit to speak to me. Nine times out of ten it will be a hymn, and suddenly a line will come to mind that perfectly answers my question, or calms my fear.

I happened to be sitting on the stand since I was the chorister that day. As I took the sacrament, a line from a pop song came into my mind. It was the song "Meant to Be" by Bebe Rexha. I was startled that a pop song came into my mind so strongly, and while I was at peace taking the sacrament. But then I realized that in my mind, there had been a word change to the line. The line talks about how *if* something is meant to be, it will happen. However, as it was playing in my head that day the words were: *when* it's meant to be, then it will be. I knew and felt in that moment that this was my message from God. He can only call to our remembrance from things that are already there. This helped me want to be better at listening to good things and reading good things, so that God has a lot He can use to talk to me. But the message was clear that day. I don't need to worry about the "when". God is in charge of that, and it *will* happen - when it's meant to be.

Revelation

That day sitting on the stand I was guided to not take any specific action, but to be at peace with where I was at. You might be given very different direction. You might feel inspired to do more online dating or enroll in an institute class with the intention of meeting people. But for me, the thing that gives me the most peace, is to let things go. Trust that when it's meant to be, it will be. I have had people near me say that I can't just sit around and wait for it to happen. I must be more actively pursuing it. But when I try to take this advice, a lot of the time I just get anxious and frustrated. However, when I work hard at trying to trust that the Lord will let me know what action to take and when to do it, I am so much happier. Whatever your revelation is, that is what you should do.

Patiently waiting isn't easy. Following God's direction isn't always the easy path. I would like to feel like I am doing *something* to make this goal happen. But the more I let go of wanting it in my timing, the more peace I feel. I am free to move forward with my life with this "let it go" attitude, which has inspired me to pursue things like building businesses and becoming a foster mom. If I was so obsessed with trying to get married, I wouldn't be pursuing and enjoying these other things that I know God wants me to do.

It Will Be Worth The Wait

When expectations are more important than the actual result, there are major issues.
For some women it is so important to be married by a certain time, that the man they marry doesn't matter. This happened to a best friend from high school. She was so focused on being the first one married, that she married the first guy she dated after high school. She tried hard to make it work for years. But eventually it was best to split up. I'm grateful she did- it wasn't a good situation.

Another friend of mine told me that when she started dating her now ex-husband, it ruined a friendship because he dated one of her best friends before they got together. She felt so guilty about it, that she thought it would be a terrible thing to break up with him after losing the friendship, and ended up marrying the guy.

Worrying about others' expectations or the expectation that marriage has to happen in a certain amount of time… can cloud the vision of what is really right.

Now I've definitely had people tell me that I must be too picky, or I'm looking for perfection, and that's why I'm not married. This of course is not fair- just like any judgment is not fair. Do not get down on yourself if someone says your expectations are too high or that you must be too picky. There might be a few women with that issue, but I believe the majority are not in that boat.

Personally, despite relatives thinking I am picky, I tend to be on the opposite side of the spectrum. At one point, I was so desperate to get married that I tried to make a relationship work even though there were things I couldn't stand about the guy. To my great benefit, he was the one who called it off. It was probably because he could tell I wasn't interested in him, despite my telling him that I was. It only took a week of not being with him to be so relieved and grateful. I shudder to think that I was so desperate to get married that I might have gone through with that and ended up with an unhappy marriage or divorce. A happy eternal marriage is worth the wait, no matter what relatives or other people may say to you.

Live Life Now

Despite not having desires and expectations met on your timeline, choose to love life *now*. It can be a hard choice, and it can take a lot of work and practice, but you can find a lot of happiness in doing so.

I'm still working on this, but I've come a long way. Sometimes the thing that helps me is making a list of the things I did well that day. I often do this in my journal. It helps me see how productive I have been, and the good things I have done. For some reason it is easy to think that I wasted a day or that I am not doing anything good. But when I write things down that I did, I realize "oh yeah, I totally did all that stuff! That's not too bad!" Sometimes you've really got to *let* yourself be happy with where you are and with what you are doing *right now*. The future can seem big and scary and the word *how* can seem so daunting and important. The way to battle being overwhelmed by the future is by being happy and grateful right now. Not how you anticipate feeling *after* you do everything. Right now.

It can be -and is - so exciting to have so many options and opportunities as a single person. You can go anywhere, whenever you want, eat ice cream for dinner, stay up way too late, sleep in as long as you want on Saturdays, and make last-minute plans. There are definitely people that tell me I am lucky to be in this position. It is satisfying to build a business, travel to foreign countries, sing in an *a cappella* group, and do so many of the other awesome things I do.

I would give it all up in a heartbeat to be married. There are days when I feel like I would do anything to make that happen. All those fabulous opportunities, goals, and even dreams take second place- a distant second place- to wanting to be a wife and mother to my own kids. But what are my options: Sit around and cry about it, or live my life the best I can, enjoying every part. One of the greatest gifts we have is agency, so we get to choose how our life will be!

Rachel A.'s Story

In my family, people get married and more importantly, people get married young. My paternal grandparents got engaged while my grandfather was serving his mission; my great-grandmother gave an engagement ring to my grandmother on behalf of my grandfather. My maternal grandparents married after four years of dating but considering they met when my grandmother was sixteen, that is still quite young. My own parents were engaged on the weekend of my father's mission homecoming and married three months later. And so, I always expected the same for myself. I would go to BYU, meet someone to marry there and together start a family.

So, when I graduated BYU very single, I truly had to start facing the reality that my life was going to be different than I imagined. To say I had mixed feelings about it would be an understatement. Here's what I wrote about it in my blog back then:

"Yes, I left BYU unmarried. No, I don't get my money back. :) Really though, I have very ambivalent feelings about this. Sometimes, I'm thrilled. I beat the system. All my friends told me

Expectations

I'd go to BYU and get married and waste everything that I ever was. I didn't agree with the idea that getting married would be a waste, but it could have changed my path in life. I had so many opportunities because I was only responsible for myself. I went to London. I played hard. I made wonderful friends. I have a degree that I love. And I get to go get my Master's degree. But sometimes, it honestly makes me sad. And scared. If I couldn't find a husband with 15,000 eligible bachelors around me what makes me think I ever will? If no one wanted me then, why would they want me now? Crazy thoughts like that come into my head. And I have to make decisions like where to go to grad school and I don't want to make them by myself. And I get lonely. And frustrated. And annoyed. I hated BYU dating culture 9 times out of 10. It's a game that I'm tired of playing. Or failing at. Whatever. But at the same time. I actually didn't play it, I chose not to. No NCMOs for me. No Premies or Dear Johns. No cliches. And I like that. Like a lot. So blah. I don't know how I feel about it. And now you know that I don't know how I feel about it."

Something key from this post was the line "I have to make decisions... and I don't want to make them by myself." Not only did I not want to make decisions by myself, if I'm being fully honest, I had created a lot of narratives about who gets to do things and when. So not only did I not want to make these decisions by myself, but I also really didn't believe that I was allowed, capable, worthy, ready, deserving. I believed that buying a house, buying nice appliances, buying nice home decor, buying a big bed, these are all things you wait and do when you're married. Starting traditions around traveling, holidays, photographs were all things I thought I had to wait for.

My dad started challenging these assumptions almost immediately when he suggested that I purchase a home in Las Vegas rather than renting somewhere. It was 2011 and the market was still quite devastated from the housing crash so financially it was an excellent decision. But I pushed back, who was I to be buying a home? I was single, I was alone, I was transient, I wasn't committed to staying in Las Vegas longer than my degree, I didn't know a lot about home maintenance. I'm so grateful that my dad dismissed each of my arguments as faulty. Being single didn't mean I wasn't deserving of a good financial decision. Being alone didn't mean I couldn't navigate the responsibility. Being transient didn't mean that this opportunity should be passed on and that I couldn't problem solve later if I wanted something different. Being inexperienced didn't mean I couldn't learn about maintaining my home. And so in August 2011, I signed my name over and over again on the paperwork to become the owner of a three bedroom condo.

  To say I was less than overwhelmed would be lying. Even with my parents' support and confidence, I was terrified by the load of things required of me by my home ownership. Getting utilities arranged, finding roommates, choosing and purchasing a couch were all massive steps for me. Then more and more experiences. The sink clogged and rather than call a plumber I put my father on FaceTime and did it myself. The unit above mine flooded and I called the repair and insurance companies and negotiated what I wanted and needed for the appropriate repairs. The HOA decided that the brown blinds I had were not up to code and needed replacing with white. So, I measured the windows, went and chose replacements and installed them by myself.
I know these all seem like the things that all adults have to learn but in my world that wasn't quite how I'd framed it. Married people owned homes and did these things. And specifically, men were responsible for home maintenance issues. So being single and female, doing these things built confidence in myself that I was capable and ready to do big things.

  Beyond that though, one of my roommates taught me a wonderful lesson about not waiting when I came home from a holiday, and she'd decorated our whole apartment to feel like a HOME. I'd lived there several years but still hung on to a sense of temporary to it all - I'd buy decor when I was married, I'd start settling in when I had someone permanent to be with. And she showed me, why wait? Why not go ahead and live the life you want, to the best of your ability, now? She showed me that I was deserving of that as I am. And so, I started buying real Christmas trees and the decorations for them. I pounded nails into the walls. I started a tradition of making crafts for holidays that will be part of my forever decor.

These two ideas really came together when I moved back to Utah in 2018. I hired realtors and sold my condo and used the proceeds for a down payment on a new home. This time, while I felt the desire to have someone to share such a big decision with, I had NO doubts about if I was ready to make such a big purchase. I also used some of the money to do other things that I was ready for in my life. I bought a Queen size mattress because you don't have to be sharing with someone to have a bigger bed. I bought leather couches because I have a dog and I wanted something that would clean easily. And I decorated the home to be my own. I love Southern Utah and the walls are filled with canvasses of my favorite places. This is my place. If someone comes along that changes how or where I want to live, awesome. But I won't wait to have what I want until then. I'm capable and worthy of living a FULL life right now.

My story happens to have come at a time when the market and my personal circumstances allowed for home purchases, but it isn't that everyone needs to buy a house. The principle is what I would go back and tell my younger self: do not believe that you have to wait until you are married to do things you want and need. If you want something, go for it. Rosemary Card owns Q.Noor, a company that sells temple dresses, and I love the example she gives of this on her social media (@rosiecard) when she talks about buying herself the appliance that she was waiting to register for as a wedding gift. That's exactly it. You don't need to have a husband to have a KitchenAid. Or Christmas decorations. Or to start bringing back souvenirs from your travels. Or to make a tradition of how you want to spend your Fourth of July. Also, don't wait for a husband to learn to do things. You need to learn where the electrical panel is in your home. And how to shut off the water and gas. You can totally replace a broken disposal in the kitchen or repair a broken toilet seat. You are capable of doing the research and then walking into a car dealership and walking out with a good deal for the car you came for. One thing that I think made the biggest difference here was having people who believed in and supported me. My parents, my siblings, my friends, my mentors cheered me on the whole time and have also shown up when things were genuinely bigger than me. If I was truly alone, this would have been way harder to do. Find some safe humans and ask to have their help and advice knowing that they will also encourage you to trust yourself and your capabilities. Those are who you need in your corner.

It's still hard to be the only one responsible for my decisions, my finances, my future. That hasn't changed. I wish I could talk through a budget, weigh pros and cons, dream and plan with someone who was going to be equally invested in the outcome of a choice. But because I've learned that I am worthy, capable, ready and deserving of living fully now, I've built myself a home, a career, relationships, memories and altogether a life that I am proud of and happy in.

Chapter 5
Navigating Adulthood

"As a young single adult, I know I have a purpose. I know I have a lot to contribute, and I know that I have a lot to be grateful for. I also know that my marital status doesn't define my maturity or my level of adulthood. Every day I'm learning more, taking on more responsibilities, and being more of a grown-up" "Self-Reliance: Don't Wait to Be Happy", *Latter-day Saints* Channel, The Church of Jesus Christ of Latter-day Saints

    For some reason many people in our culture have linked marriage with being an adult. This is probably because most people used to be married before the age of 25. However, the average age for marriage is getting older and older (even in Utah). Unfortunately, in a lot of ways we still link marriage with being an adult.

    Sometimes well-meaning family are part of this issue. Family might assume that 'your husband will take care of that' when it comes to certain chores or expenses, so they don't help teach you certain skills. I have seen this happen in families with everything from finances and budgeting to buying a car, to mowing the lawn. Or, your parents might have encouraged you to pursue a great 'mom career' in your schooling, and now you are finding it hard to make a good income.

    Sometimes church leaders make it hard for you to feel like an adult. I've seen some singles ward bishoprics who love to do everything for the ward members. They run everything and don't really let anyone else take responsibilities.

    And a lot of the time single people themselves associate adulthood with marriage. I know I have. One of the first things I noticed was with my bedspread. I got one for Christmas right after high school to take with me to college. After college and a mission,

I still had that bedspread. I was getting sick of it, and wanted a new one, but I really thought it would be weird to buy one myself, especially since I'd probably get married soon, so I wouldn't need a twin bedspread for much longer anyways.

Ten years after that Christmas when I got that bedspread, I finally decided that it didn't matter if I got married in six months, I wanted my own queen size bed. I told myself that in the future it could become the bed for my husband and I, or it could become a guest bed, or I could get rid of it. By that point in my life, a twin bed was representative of a single life – alone and transient. Instead, I wanted to focus on a permanent home and long-term relationships.

It was intimidating for me to pick out exactly the bed I wanted. I tried out a number of beds and ended up really happy with my choice. I got to pick a bed that *I* loved; no one else needed to approve of it. Then, I picked out a bedspread and pillows that I would enjoy. One of my pillows is big and fuzzy and pink! I figured now is the time to do that because my husband might not appreciate pink and fuzz like I do.

It felt really good to make those decisions by myself. The only regret I have is not having done it sooner! I think it is our culture of believing that marriage and adulthood are the same things that has young adults putting things off. It can be things as small as a bedspread, or as large as a home purchase. As we choose not to put off our happiness and progress for the unknown, I believe we will enjoy the now a lot more.

It's Ok To Have A Career

One thing you can focus on is a career. Sometimes we feel guilty for working or having a demanding career because women of the church are supposed to stay home and raise a family. But did you know Utah was the first state where women had jobs that previously had only been done by men? Did you know that Utah was the first state where women got the right to vote? Women were considered property until around the time of the restoration of the church. The gospel of Jesus Christ shook off the shackles for women, and it has spread from the church to many parts of the world. We have set the example for industry and leadership for women since the dark ages. There are also scriptures in the Book of Mormon about women working (See Mosiah 10:5, Helaman 6:13).

    I truly believe that God needs me to be a leader in my field to influence many lives for good and direct people to Him. I know that if I had been married even just a few years ago, I wouldn't have had the same motivation to pursue career goals, leaving it to my husband to provide. Sometimes I tell God I don't want to be a career woman- just a mom. His plan is to allow me to be a mom- that's been promised to me. Through personal revelation though, I know He also expects me to do my very best in my career. Sometimes married friends will tell me they wish they could have had more time to focus on a career or have a business on the side to provide a feeling of accomplishment and add to the family resources. I don't think I will ever feel that way, seeing as I have been working for so many years, so it's a blessing that I will never feel like I have missed out on anything. In fact, by the time I finish my single life chapter, I will have a long list of awesome things I have learned and accomplished and am proud of. I fully plan to leave this time with absolutely no regrets because I am maximizing it!

Family Activities

    Family activities where you are a sibling can sometimes be hard when you are single. Make sure you take care of yourself during these events. One thing that can help them be more enjoyable is volunteering to plan part of it. Another thing is to lose yourself in spending time with nephews and nieces. When you are in the moment with kids, it's hard to think about much else. I like to try and think of things I can do to be prepared to help out if needed. I bring extra snacks, or if we go somewhere over night, I leave my door open at night so my nephews can come find me in the morning if their parents are still sleeping. When I feel I am contributing and helping, these times are much more enjoyable.

Even though you are single, you can still call yourself a family. You're a family of one. As a family of one, you can do family things. One thing I have learned is that I do not need to have a husband to take myself on a family vacation. I have started to take one personal family vacation a year. My favorite place to go is this gorgeous bed and breakfast in Ephraim, Utah. It even has a spa! I treat myself to a spa treatment, then I do my annual goal setting and 'family' planning. I stay just for one night. In the morning I get a fancy breakfast. After that I go visit friends, or go to the Temple, or anything I like. It's just a 24-hour trip, but it helps me feel like an adult that is living their best life, and I come back feeling more ready to take on the rest of my life.

Running Away

One thing I see a lot of women do to avoid having to face the adulting world alone is go to school. There is definitely nothing wrong with going to school, if done for the right reasons. The right reasons are for career progress or change, or a spiritual prompting. School can be a door to progress and opportunities.

However, if you are just unsure about what to do with your life, there are many other things you can do besides wrack up school loans. Especially if school just isn't your thing, you'd be much better off finding internships or job shadowing opportunities or starting a business to gain experience and expertise.

Going to school to date is a very expensive thing to do, and will potentially make you unhappy because you will spend a lot of energy studying when you really wanted to be dating. If dating is your goal, why not try dating apps? That is cheaper than going to school, and with so many people on them these days you will likely be able to find people to date. Or you can move to a new city without going to school.

I was led to start a business when I was 25 years old. As I began building it up, the work became really difficult. I thought a lot about going to grad school. I tried to convince myself that going to grad school would help me with my business, but really I had plenty of mentorship around me already. I was just trying to get myself out of doing the hard work of getting a business started. I am glad I ended up not going back to school, and stuck it out. I've gained so many wonderful connections and experience through my work that I may not have had, had I run away from those opportunities.

Be A Mom Now

When Eve was given her name, she was called "the mother of all living" even before she had birthed a child. There are ways to be a mom in our communities, families, and to those in need. I have found great satisfaction in this work.

A couple of years ago I asked myself: If I had all the time and money in the world, what would I do with it? The answer at the time surprised me: I'd spend more time with my nephews. What a simple thing. I didn't have to wait for more time and money, I could do that now! Since then, I have taken every Friday afternoon off to play with my two nephews and now my two nieces as well. I cherish this time with them. I get to know them more, and we create memories. Every year for Christmas I give them a book with pictures and written memories from the year. I know they appreciate the fun we have, but I appreciate it probably more than they do! It fills a hole in my heart.

There are so many wonderful women serving like this. I have an aunt who didn't get married until later. Instead of closing herself off from her sisters with kids, she became our favorite aunt. My cousins and I all have fond memories of sleepovers at her house, and getting to job shadow her for school projects, going skiing with her, learning how to draw from her, learning about how to be healthy, and more. She has been an example and inspiration to me.

From the time I was in high school I knew I wanted to be a foster mom one day. When I got back from my mission, I learned that you can become a foster parent if you are single as long as you are 21 years old, and have the space for it- you don't even have to own your own home. I thought about it a bit, but I figured I would be married first. As time went by, I found myself a home owner without being married, and this gave me the space to become a foster mom. I decided to take a leap and do it!

It takes some time to become a foster parent. You take classes, have interviews, and have to have your house prepared. It is a difficult job to prepare for and do, and it is not high paying- mostly enough to cover things like clothes and food for the child. But there is a need for it to be done, and it can bless your life in amazing ways.

I had the privilege of being a foster mom to a 15-year-old teenage girl for a year. I was not expecting it to fill me up like it did. It was a dream come true driving through the parent carpool lane to drop her off and pick her up every day at the high school. I loved planning a birthday party, giving her Christmas presents, and making green pancakes for breakfast on Saint Patrick's Day for her. I was even delighted any time she asked for help with homework!

As a foster mom, I never wanted to adopt while single. Here in Utah, only one out of five children need adoption, as we focus more on reunification as this seems to help most kids succeed long term. I figured I'd be a good stopping place for kids that need it while their parents get back on their feet. However, my daughter ended up being the one in five. I was not expecting to be asked if I was open to adoption. That was hard. I ultimately decided to help in the process of finding her a permanent home, but chose not to take that option myself. It nearly broke my heart, so I have decided not to take in another kid just yet.

Foster care is not something for everyone. Especially while single, being able to make it work with school or daycare schedules can be very challenging. The nice thing is you can let them know what ages you feel you can take. For example, I said kids ages 8-19, since I would need to work while they were in school, and eight seemed about the youngest I'd be able to handle personally. However, the biggest thing is being able to handle the ups and downs of your heart. I think the time I had with my daughter was exactly what each of us needed. As hard as it was, I am so grateful and fulfilled inside because of the time we spent together. I hope to do a lot more work in foster care in the future because there are a lot of kids that need it. But I know I need to be in a place mentally and emotionally that I can do it again.

There are other ways to serve as a mom in the community. You can volunteer to read to kids, and lots of cities have big brother/big sister programs that allow you to mentor adolescent and young adults that need support. If there is a part of you in your adulthood that craves to be a mom, you can find ways to do it without being married.

Overwhelm

Married or not, I think there are hard parts to being an adult. One of the biggest difficulties is dealing with overwhelm. Single people can get hit hard with this because they get to wear all the hats- from provider to cook, to lawn mower, to laundry do-er. As I have worked on navigating overwhelm, there are some things I have learned that have been very helpful.

Tip one is to prioritize. Make a list of everything on your mind. Now divide it into what must be done today, and what doesn't. Put the things that must be done today at the top of your list. The other things can be written farther down your list, or write them on the to-do list for another day.

Tip two is to break it down. Let's say there is an email that I need to click on and respond to, but I really don't want to for whatever reason. I might break it down this way: Today I will click on it and read it. Tomorrow I will work on my response, and the next day I will actually respond. I have a to-do list for each day on my Google calendar, and I will actually write these three separate steps on each to-do list for today, tomorrow, and the next day.

Tip three is to put things away mentally. This can be done after you make your game plan from tip two. Basically what it means to put it away is you tell yourself you are not allowed to think about that thing until it is time to pull out your to-do list again. Sometimes there are big things that aren't coming for a couple of weeks that maybe you are dreading. The best way I know of to deal with this, is actually put a time and date on my calendar for when I am allowed to think about this thing. Until that day, I'm not allowed to let it worry or upset me. This has been a life changing thing for me to do.

Decision Making

Making big decisions is hard. Things like deciding where to live or where to work is often a difficult thing for all adults, married or single. But when you are single, making some big decisions can feel like you are giving up on marriage. For example: you never wanted to buy a home while single. It was never part of the plan. And yet, sometimes it feels like the right thing to do, or you want to do it even though there is no man in sight yet. I am here to tell you that doing big things is not giving up. You are allowing yourself to progress, and doing big adulting things will not make it so you are less likely to get married.

My sister and I bought our first house together when I was 27 and she was 26. It was really nice having someone to go in on it with. I have lots of single gal friends that get condos or town homes on their own, though. For myself and everyone I talk to that has done this, it is intimidating at first. Even when you sign the papers you kind of have a bit of fear just because it is such a big commitment. But something I realized is that marriage is an even bigger commitment, so it's good practice!

Buying a home is simply a matter of knowing the requirements, then checking off the boxes. You can go to a mortgage lender and ask them what you need to do to qualify. I first did this a year or two before buying a home so that I could be ready. It's free to do that, and then you can make sure you set yourself up for success. Being a homeowner is a lot of work, but it is also very satisfying. I've met a lot of single women who would like to own a home and don't realize that they are closer than they think!

There are lots of other decisions you can make besides buying a home, like staying with a job or living in a new place. The thing that makes it hard is wanting to be in the right place at the right time for when Mr. Right comes along. I believe though, that God isn't going to let you miss your husband. Especially if you are trying to follow your heart, grow your gifts and talents, and become the best person you can be with the decisions you make. I believe that as you follow the Spirit and your heart, the right people and experiences will be attracted to you.

It's Not All Bad

Adulting is not all bad. Sometimes it can be fun and give you great satisfaction. Once I became a homeowner, I had to learn a whole set of new skills. I had never mowed a lawn before. I had always assumed my husband would do that, since my dad always did that growing up. But suddenly I had my own yard, and no husband. So, I learned how to mow a lawn. Now it is one of my most favorite things to do! I love a newly mowed lawn, especially if I did it! Sometimes I will let it grow longer than a week, just so that when I do mow it, there is a drastic difference. It's so satisfying!

There have been little things that come up now and then: leaks, fridge lights, microwave handles. It's not my favorite thing to do these repairs, and sometimes I need to call in a professional. But

I am always proud of myself after completing a necessary task, and feel good about my work, even if the new hook on the wall is a bit crooked. Hey, I put it up myself!

What To Do When You Don't Feel Treated Like An Adult

It can be hard to know how to handle situations where you don't feel treated appropriately for your age or level of experience. It can be off-putting and embarrassing. Take a deep breath. The person who made the comment probably has never been in your shoes. It is ok to point out how you are feeling. Sharing your feelings and trying to help the person understand you better will only improve your relationship.

Oftentimes for me the right thing to say doesn't come up in the moment. Instead of just getting angry about it, I try and take time to collect my thoughts and then call or write a note to the person. This helps the other person know what it feels like when they say certain things, and we both end up in a better place because of it.

Navigating adulthood is not always easy. But just because you are married it isn't going to magically get easier. Knowing how to budget, take care of a house, or pay taxes don't just happen when a person gets married. I know plenty of married people that need a lot of help adulting too. It's skills we all need to develop, and you can do it while single. You might even really enjoy it!

Mallory M.'s Story

When I arrived at BYU at 18 years old, I came with a single goal in mind; find the man of my dreams (preferably sooner rather than later), get married, have a family, and live out the rest of my days as a stay-at-home mom. That is how it had been done by my mother and my grandmother before her, and my great-grandmother before her. Education was important, but in my mind, it was the thing you did in the background while you waited to find your future spouse. I had enjoyed an idyllic childhood filled with memorable traditions and close-knit extended family relationships, and I couldn't wait to create my own little world where I could pass all of it on to future generations. Never in my wildest dreams could I have guessed that at 28, I would be single and living in Europe while I finished a PhD and prepared for a career in academia. Never in my wildest dreams could I have imagined how happy and fulfilled that kind of life could make me feel.

But as you can guess, learning how to navigate being single post-college in the LDS culture is no cakewalk. It hasn't always been a happy and fulfilling journey. In fact, many times it can feel like the lows outweigh the highs. One challenge facing many post-college single adults is that elements of the culture seem to create a period of eternal adolescence for singles, where their adulthood isn't fully recognized by parents, church leaders, or married peers. It can feel demeaning to watch others be given responsibilities and opportunities for growth while you are passed up simply because of your marital status. In my life, this has been manifested in the times that I have been seated with the teenagers or younger cousins at a wedding instead of with my same-aged married peers or passed over when the food assignments for family get-togethers are given out as if being single means you haven't quite reached the level of responsibility necessary to be given an assignment. When I first moved to Europe at age 27, I even had a bishop invite me to attend Young Women's activities instead of seeing me as an adult worthy of a calling like the married 27-year-olds (one of which was the Young Women's president). Most of my post-college single friends can tell similar stories. However, I don't share these stories to be discouraging. Rather, my goal is to highlight the difficulty that can be created by a cultural belief that equates marriage with adulthood. It has been my experience that learning to separate those two constructs (and learning to separate marriage from other young adult goals and dreams) can open a pathway to happiness and fulfillment in the lives in LDS single adults in addition to providing more realistic expectations for future marriages.

Pretty soon after arriving at BYU as a freshman, I met a guy who in my mind was "the full package". He was everything I thought I wanted in a future partner and more. However, I very quickly became aware that I was not yet the type of person who could be an equal partner to that kind of guy. I had a lot of growing and personal development that I needed to do. So, I made it my personal mission to put in the necessary work to become that type of person so that the next time a guy like that came around, I would be ready. This seemed to fit with the counsel given over the pulpit to many young single adults to "become" the type of person that you would want to marry. However, this council would soon become problematic for me, as what first started out as a quest for personal development soon turned into a perfectionist drive to prove myself worthy of love and acceptance. As the years passed and the opportunity for marriage still didn't present itself, I believed that it must be because I had one more thing I needed to "fix" about myself or one more lesson God needed to teach me before I would be "ready". Subconsciously, I had tied my own self-acceptance to whether or not I was married. It took another wonderful guy walking in and out of my life for me to realize that I *had* become the type of person who could be an equal partner to the kind of man I was looking for, but that type of guy would never see that in me if I couldn't see it in myself.

With that realization came many more. Not only had I tied my self-acceptance to being married, but as was mentioned earlier, I had let the culture attach my ability to reach adulthood to my marital status. Though I craved the companionship that comes with being married, I was equally looking to marriage to make me independent in the eyes of my peers. On top of that, I had even made smaller desires like feeling the satisfaction of having my own place conditional upon my being married. Allowing so many of my other needs and desires to hinge on my getting married (something that often felt largely out of my control) created an intense amount of pressure around dating that often led to anxiety or discouragement. Not only that, it made me feel stuck, like none of the things I really needed to continue to progress with my life were actually accessible to me. When so much of your happiness depends on the "right" person coming into your life, it can be easy to start feeling bitterness towards God for not miraculously sending them your way.

 Luckily, while I was engaged in the battle to "become" the type of person I would want to marry, I was also pursuing my education, and I discovered my talent and passion for researching the process of human development. I was also developing my relationship with God and learning little by little to trust him with the direction of my life. Even if it meant bringing my feelings of anger and bitterness directly to Him and letting him teach me to sit with them and process them. It was the combination of these things that led me to pursue a PhD and I was soon accepted at a University in the Netherlands. Moving away from Utah where the LDS culture is most prevalent was the step that I needed to be able to see that I could achieve my desire of being independent and recognized as an adult without being married. As I was continually vulnerable with God and trusted him with my honest thoughts and feelings, He taught me how to separate my self-acceptance and self-worth from marriage as well. Gradually, I began to see that so much of what I was looking for and dreaming of can be achieved as I am now, and that thought is incredibly freeing. There are days when I still feel the ache of loneliness, and I still hope to be married someday, but I am living a much more fulfilling life now that I understand that my happiness is not conditional upon marriage. I can envision a very happy future for myself as a single person, filled with friends and family, a career and hobbies that I love, and plenty of time to give myself to the service of God. For the first time in my life, instead of holding so much space for the

Moving Forward

"what-ifs" and trying to plan my "now" around it, I am wholeheartedly embracing my "now" so that if a "what-if" meets me along the road, it can only add to the beauty I have already created for myself.

Chapter 6
Progress When You Feel Stuck

"Look for opportunities to expand your mind and your skills…Involve the Lord in your efforts, and He will guide you…The more you learn, the more you can help build God's kingdom and influence the world for good."– "For the Strength of Youth Pamphlet", The Church of Jesus Christ of Latter-day Saints.

It is easy to spend too much time focusing on not being married and think that I am not improving much and that I am wasting these years. But when I read journal entries from a year ago, I am always surprised to see so much progress!

For example, throughout the years I have struggled to be a positive and happy person. I didn't think I had improved much in this until I read through my mission journals three years later. I was so negative back then! I was constantly writing negative things about myself or talking about how horrible I was at being a missionary. Reading it years later, I was surprised at just how mean I was to myself! Then I felt grateful for my improvement. I no longer treat myself so badly. Thanks to my journal writing, I was able to see progress.

If I Was Married Then…

One of the most interesting phone conversations I have ever had was with a guy I was in love with on the other side of the world. We hadn't talked much in about a year. It was too hard to do the long-distance thing so we had let it go. But then we started texting again just a little bit. That then turned into a phone conversation. During the call he started to get a little upset and ended by saying something along the lines of: "You're the reason I haven't pursued more education- because I never knew if I was staying in my country or going to yours!"

After he said that, I clarified by asking: "So it is *my* fault you don't have more advanced degrees or education?" to which he replied "yes". This was mind blowing to me. He was blaming me for his lack of progress in life.

It might be tempting to simply assume he was a bad egg. But many single women think in a similar way: "If I was married then….", fill in the blank. So many of us have pushed off life, spending our time continually waiting for marriage. When this goal isn't fulfilled, we look for people or things to blame. We might think that God doesn't love us, or that the unfairness of our situation or relationships are to blame. We might even blame ourselves.

This kind of thinking is not just unproductive; it is untrue. Perhaps you are meant to be like Rachel in the Bible, who had to wait 14 years for her husband Jacob. This wasn't because there was anything wrong with her, or because God didn't love her. It was simply not the time for that life chapter.

How did Rachel live those 14 years? I'd love to know. When she first met Jacob, her father Laban said Jacob would have to work for him for seven years to earn Rachel's hand. So he did. But on the wedding night, Jacob discovered he had married Rachel's older sister Leah. When he went back to Laban and demanded to know what happened, Laban just responded: "It must not be so done… to give the younger before the firstborn" (Genesis 29:26). Did Rachel know this would happen? Obviously, Jacob wasn't expecting this. If I was Rachel, I would have been worried that Jacob wouldn't want anything to do with me after what had happened. And then Laban tells Jacob if he wants Rachel too, he's going to have to work another seven years! How hard that must have been for both of the lovers. Did she waste away her days sighing and wishing, and crying to God that life wasn't fair? Or did she learn skills, become closer to God, and build herself as a person? Well, we really don't know.

We do know that after she was married, she then wasn't able to have children for a long time. Her sister had four babies, and Leah and Rachel's handmaids who they gave to Jacob to marry as well all had children before Rachel ever got pregnant.

Rachel's life was full of waiting and sometimes she found it hard to be patient. At one point she says to Jacob, "Give me children, or else I die." (Genesis 30:1) We think it's bad in our day to be single and childless. In Rachel's day, people often assumed you were a sinner or there was something wrong with you if you didn't have kids! What kept her going? What kept her progressing? What kept her close to the Lord? She was Jacob's favorite wife. It's hard to believe that would be the case if she was always moping around and feeling sorry for herself.

I don't know what Rachel did to be happy and stay strong through her trials, but there are some things I have learned and seen throughout my life. A big part is taking ownership of my life. Your life doesn't start when you marry. It started when you were born, and we only get one chance to live. My attitude through most of my singleness has been: If I've got to be single, I might as well have the best single life I possibly can!

It's Ok To Be Amazing

Elder Ballard in the April 2021 General Conference gave a very powerful talk for the empowerment of single people in the church. He explains that some things won't be set right until the Millennium, "but that doesn't mean that every blessing is deferred until the Millennium; some have already been received, and others will continue to be received until that day". Something I consider to be a blessing right now is my time and freedom.

Most days I really don't like sleeping in. I'd much rather be awake. But on Saturdays especially I realized after a time that I felt *guilty* if I slept in. I thought this was strange… but as I pondered it, I realized I felt guilty because if I had kids, I wouldn't be able to sleep in! That was a weird realization for me. How did I get to that point subconsciously? I'm not totally sure. One thing I do know is that I worked on fixing it as soon as I realized what I was doing. It was all in the mentality. I had to think: there are pros to being married and a mom, but there are pros to being single too, and it's ok to enjoy them!! Sleeping- especially as long as you want without the interruptions of children- is definitely one of the biggest pros we've got!

A couple of years ago I was seeing a lot of development and progress in myself. This was especially happening in business and career areas. It was exciting, but then I began to worry... What if I get too far ahead, and then no guy will want to date me? What if I am too intimidating to date as a successful career woman? I didn't need any more barriers to dating. I thought to myself that as much as I enjoy business and careers and leadership, I'd much rather have a family. I thought maybe I should step back from my career, and try to patiently wait for a guy before trying to reach my potential.

Around that time, I received a Father's Priesthood blessing for health reasons. The blessing said something along the lines of: "Don't hold yourself back from pursuing your best self in an effort to be more attractive. Your husband will be equal to you". I hadn't mentioned anything about my feelings on this subject to my dad, and I knew the Lord had heard my silent thoughts.

I think this is good advice to all single women. Don't hold yourself back from pursuing dreams and goals. God knows your heart. As you grow closer to Him and know how to hear His voice, He will direct you. If marriage is not meant to happen for a while, you'll only have regrets if you wasted all of that time. You can be always anxiously engaged in good causes. Another way of thinking about it is you've got to be moving for God to direct your path! God can't steer a parked car. It's ok to try things, grow, and build.

I once had a conversation with a single friend, and she thought that maybe the reason she and others are single longer is because they have important work to do that would be hard to pursue as a mom. Maybe not having a family yet is a little blessing from God, giving you permission to pursue other passions, ideas, or develop skills. This friend is an artist, and her work is incredible. Of course, a mom can still paint. But there are definitely more barriers to doing that if you are also trying to run a family. Maybe God needs her to develop these talents- they will do so much good in the world, and He needs her to really focus on that right now. Eventually her time will be focused on a family, but she will also have completed the work God needed her to do while single. I really like this thought- that God sees these other desires inside of us and wants to give us opportunities to pursue them. We might discover things that make us super happy and fulfilled that we would be unable to do as a mom.

What Are You Supposed To *Do* While Single?

One December I spent some time contemplating and planning what I wanted to do in the coming year- what would be best to do. I wasn't sure. There were quite a few things I wanted to work on, things I wanted to accomplish but I wanted to do what was 'right'.

After about three weeks of pondering, I went to the Temple, focusing on these thoughts. I got to the Celestial room and picked up a Book of Mormon. I felt like I should open up to Words of Mormon so I did and my eyes went right to this phrase: "Wherefore, I chose these things..." (Words of Mormon 1:5). To me, that scripture was revelation. It was God telling me that I could do the things *I* chose to do. Why not? I am His daughter, a noble daughter of the Most High King. If I took that title seriously, what would I be doing with my life? Wouldn't I be doing all the wonderful things I wanted to do? Wouldn't I be trying to shine a light into the world and lift others and accomplish all my dreams and be amazing? I felt so empowered, as if I could take on any challenge and do anything! And it was because God was helping me embrace agency. There have definitely been times in my life where I am frustrated that God won't give me the exact steps to what I should do. But as I have learned to love myself more, trust in Him more, and learn who I am, this has been such a powerful thing to learn. I can do anything I choose! I can do *all* the things I want to do, because I was born to be great.

Find your Passion

One of my favorite talks is Elder Uchdorf's: "Happiness, Your Heritage". There's a large section of his talk dedicated to talking about how creating- anything- adds to happiness. To me it is very influential and helpful to know that everyone can create, and that we should, no matter what it is!

Maybe you are thinking, "This is great, and I do have that desire to create something! But I can't think of anything to do!" I can relate. I am a passionate and driven person, but at times I have struggled knowing what to be passionate and driven about. First of all, if you can't figure it out right now, it's ok! Stressing about not knowing what to do does not make it happen. Tell yourself it's ok, and it will happen eventually. Here are some ideas of things you can try to help you find things to be passionate about and do.

1. Read your Patriarchal Blessing. In chapter 2 of the *Gospel Principles* manual, it says, "We were not all alike in heaven... We possessed different talents and abilities, and we were called to do different things on earth. We can learn more about our 'eternal possibilities' when we receive our patriarchal blessings (see Thomas S. Monson, in Conference Report, Oct. 1986, 82; or *Ensign*, Nov. 1986, 66)." Your Patriarchal Blessing will show you things the Lord expects you to develop and work on.
2. Pay attention to what makes you happy. Don't stake your happiness only on dating and marriage. For right now, figure out what *else* makes you happy.
3. Pay attention to what keeps you up at night. What do you think about? Are there any ideas that form? Keep a notepad by your bed just in case. Don't become

discouraged if nothing comes. It might take many nights of trying.
4. Clear out thought 'garbage' that could be blocking the thoughts you want to be having. Negative thoughts, obsessions, or addictions could be blocking the flow of creativity. Do your best to clear these from your mind. I imagine taking my thoughts, crumpling them up, and putting them outside my bedroom door. With those worrying thoughts out of the way, I can meditate or journal.
5. Ask for a Priesthood blessing. Get divine help to know what to do to head in the best direction for you.
6. Take out a notebook and do a journaling exercise. Ask yourself these questions: If you had a million dollars, and all the time in the world, what would you do? What would you donate to? What would you start? Who would you help?
7. Is there a talent you wish you had? Why not actually sign up for lessons and learn how to do that thing? Yes, it costs money. A lot of good things in life do. Instead of buying that new outfit, or getting your nails done, you could invest in a talent for yourself.
8. One of the most important lessons I have ever learned in life is about the motivation myth (Jeff Haden wrote a book about this; it contains strong language.). So many of us believe we have to *feel* like doing something before we do it. This is simply not how life works. Many times we have to start doing something and then the motivation will come. Start something you want to be passionate about and see if the passion comes in the doing.
9. Ask your parents about the things that you loved doing as a kid, and what you were like. That might give you some insight into what you would love to do now.
10. Interview people you know who are passionate about what they do. Watch how their countenances change as they

describe what they love. Take notes on their discovery journey and see if you get ideas on finding and pursuing passions.
11. Be a bit reckless. Try things you haven't done before and that push you out of your comfort zone and be open to changes and new ideas. You might find a new passion and you will very likely have experiences that help you learn and grow.

Just do it

Maybe you don't have a desire to create something, but you're tired of feeling like life is meaningless and you are drowning in existential grief. Most single women have felt they cannot progress without being married. It's the natural next step in life, and it can seem like you are getting left behind if it isn't happening. Elder Renlund's talk, "Infuriating Unfairness" from the April 2021 conference, has some helpful counsel. He said: "For us to insist on knowing *how* or *when* is unproductive and, after all, myopic." So instead of focusing on the how and when of getting married, we can focus on personal growth and happiness. There are many things you can do that are productive and fulfilling even as you continue hoping for a different future. Here are some ideas…

Arts

Even if you're not artistic, paint a picture. One time when I was struggling with life, my sister brought over large poster paper, a bunch of finger paint, and Q-tips. I'm not a gifted artist like she is, but that day I pretended to be an artist too. My painting of a scene in my favorite Chilean city didn't turn into quite the masterpiece I had envisioned. In fact, it was not that great. But you know what? I enjoyed doing it anyway! I posted it on my wall like a little kid, and it made me feel proud of myself every time I looked at it.

Learn an instrument.
There was a time when I really just wanted to learn how to play the guitar. I would think about it sometimes. But it seemed like a lot of work, and my fingers are so short and squatty I just never allowed myself to go there. But one day I was like, "I'm tired of not fulfilling this desire!" And instead of wishing to play, I grabbed my roommate's guitar and learned using youtube. It was hard, but not nearly as bad as I thought it would be.

Learn a language.
Being able to speak another language can change your life. A language affects how people think. It is a huge part of how a culture develops. Jokes rarely translate from one language to another. It's just how culture and language work. Being able to speak the language of the place you travel to is a huge confidence booster. If you are one of those people desperate to travel, but it makes you nervous, do something practical like learn the language of the place you want to go. This will build your confidence and you are much more likely to actually go to that place.

Education
Get certified in something that interests you. I once got an online certification to teach English as a second language when I was considering living out of the country for a while. I had to get certified in CPR to become a foster mom. I recommend finding something you like that might require certification and trying it out. Be mentored in something that interests you. In the Church, we understand how important education is. But this doesn't mean you need to go to college. I love these lines from the "For the Strength of Youth" pamphlet: "Look for opportunities to expand your mind and your skills. These opportunities can include formal education at school or vocational training as well as informal learning from sources your trust". College is helpful for lots of people, and if you want to do that and can, do it.
But what I want to stress is not overlooking other opportunities. There are people who you can connect with, who are willing to

give you direction. There are life coaches, seminars, and online classes. When I began working in financial services, I had no idea super successful people would give me advice and teach me about business, success, relationships, and more. But I took the initiative to learn about finances and get licensed. Now I have close contact with super successful financial mentors who teach me all sorts of things about life and money. It's awesome. It wasn't college, but it has been incredibly educational. You can learn just as much or more than you would in college by going to events or classes (online or in-person) and connecting with experts in things that interest you. It can be professional, like my financial classes, or it can be about a hobby or other interest.

Sometimes I count authors as my mentors. For example, I count Kristen Oaks, wife of Dallin H. Oaks, as my mentor. That's because the spirit led me to read her book, "A Single Voice" a number of years ago. I felt that I was led to that book in miraculous ways, and it helped me to see the positive of being single- I'm sure it's part of the reason why the idea to write this book came to me. If you can find a mentor you can interact with, and they can observe what you are doing and give you timely advice, that's ideal. But I love my book mentors as well. The biggest thing I learned from her was that being single is not something to be simply endured. There is beauty and purpose to it. There are blessings in this time!

Finances

Learn money management skills. If there is one skill you will never regret learning, it is managing money and budgeting! Finances are one of the top reasons for divorce, so do your future family a favor and learn how to be good at this. It is a skill that will serve you and them your whole life.

Self-development Reading

Read a self-development book, or a book about something that really interests you that is nonfiction. For this kind of reading, it is better to read just five pages a day and take notes, than read it cover to cover as quickly as you can.

Health
Learning how to eat and live healthy is a great skill to develop as a future mom. I was so intimidated to make food for my foster daughter when she first came. It was stressful figuring out how to grocery shop and set aside time to cook and then actually make food. It was a whole new level to then try and make sure I was giving her proper nutrition. It took time and practice but eventually I figured out how to do it in a way that I liked, and since then I have enjoyed learning about nutrition. It makes me feel great for myself, and I am excited to bless my family with my knowledge in this area one day.
Gardening can be a part of this too if you live in a place with the space to do so. There's something so satisfying about bringing plants into life and creating beauty and/or food. Garden vegetables are much better than any you can get from the store!

Career
Building a career brings a lot of satisfaction. Some careers require degrees, but many do not- or it doesn't matter what your degree was in. Every woman that I have met that has a job that she likes is happier because of it- married or not. When you are working in a career, you really feel like you are contributing and making a difference. This is a big deal because most people work 40 hours a week. That's a long time to just be doing something that isn't helping you to grow or to feel like you are contributing. Even if you feel like you are just waiting to get married, find work that allows you to grow and progress. You never know if you might need (or want) to help financially with your family in the future, so the benefits won't end after you marry.

Start a business.
If you feel like you have an idea that needs to be shared with the world, *go for it!* If you've got a business you want to start, *just try it!*

Moving Forward

Being single is the best time for this! If you end up bombing it and 'waste' all your money, you could just go live in your parents' basement for a while. You don't affect your kids' lives or anything like that. Think of the mega life experiences of failing or succeeding in making a business!

Bucket List

Make a bucket list, but actually do the things on the list. This is really fun- and it is satisfying and fulfilling. I hate saying, "we should do that sometime", unless I know I will really follow through with it. Life is more fun when you actually follow through with the things you want to do.

Here's something that can help with this. Every time you catch yourself saying, "I wish I could…" or "I really want to…" write it down and put it on your wall. Then, make plans to do that thing and actually do it. When your time of being single is over, you can look back at great memories instead of thinking, "I really wish I would have…"

Just for Fun

Learn random things for fun when you are bored. I have learned how to make balloon animals and tap dance. You don't have to be perfect or even good at these things. Just try something and if you like it, keep doing it! My sister has learned to juggle and do a Rubix Cube. If you ever find yourself feeling like you are boring or have nothing to say when someone asks what your skills or hobbies are, this is the perfect idea for you. Also, if you feel overqualified with your hobbies or skills, learn something silly too. I love telling people that I can beatbox. Then I always have to show them which of course breaks the ice in any situation from a formal dinner to a carnival date. Loosening up and learning things that aren't seen as useful is very rewarding, fun, and will serve you well as a single person.

Plan Your Time

Sometimes getting started is the hardest part of any project. I have found that it helps me to do weekly planning. Sunday night or Monday morning I try to come up with a list of things I want to do for the week and plan out my time. I think about things I really want to do and my goals for the year; then I decide what I'm going to do that week to accomplish those. I write those things down in my planner. As I write, I picture who I will be by the end of the week- how I will have grown from Sunday to Sunday. When I do this, I am much more likely to get things done that are most important to me, instead of wasting my time.

When I need a little jump start- I really just want to lay on the couch and watch YouTube or scroll on social media -I have found that doing something else first for just 10 minutes helps. I tell myself: just take 10 minutes to go on a walk, or clean something. After those 10 minutes, I can relax. This works really well when I struggle to find motivation. Sometimes after the 10 minutes, I feel like I can do more things. Other times I really do need to relax, but at least I feel a little better that I did something productive first. Rest days are good, but I have found that a rest *hour* feels better and more fulfilling than taking an entire day. If you like, you can alternate one-hour relaxation periods with ten-minute work periods. You will find you have a lot more time than you thought when you set limits and stick to them.

Making a list helps too. Even when I am bored or tired, if I have a list of things I want to do, I always find I accomplish more. Even if it is on breaks between episodes of a show, if I just check off one box between episodes, or check off a box during an episode of a show, I'm taking steps towards long-term goals and happiness even while enjoying my today.

Proper Rest

I love being busy; I get a lot of fulfillment out of *doing*. Sometimes though, I catch myself feeling like I am drowning. Even though I like all the things I am doing, it feels like it is taking over and choking me for some unknown reason. With time, I have learned that often when I feel that choking feeling, all I need to do is stop what I'm doing and take some deep breaths for a few minutes. Alternatively, if I take time to be still and meditate in the morning, I don't get this feeling of drowning during the day. The paradox of taking time to be quiet and slow down is that it makes a person more productive. It seems *unproductive* because I don't see it working until I look back and realize that I probably had a more productive day *because* I took time to meditate.

Finding the balance between not running faster than you are able, and not being lazy, can be hard. I think everyone has a different capacity to live life. When I first got back from my mission, it was really hard for me to work even 20 hours a week without breaking down emotionally. I would start crying at work and need to go home. It took time- years - to increase my capacity to work more. It's been a journey and now I am so grateful that I can work 'normal' hours. It's important to stretch ourselves and grow, but it's also important to take care of our mental, physical, and emotional health.

Slowing down and relaxing also helps me to hear God. When I am tense and frustrated, it is harder for me to hear His voice, which usually makes me even more frustrated. While some people are able to go out in nature to reset, that doesn't work well for me. But going on a walk in my neighborhood, being in my room in silence, and sitting in my car are all places that help me find stillness. Finding relaxation methods that work for you can help you hear God better. As I am able to listen to God, He helps me to feel good about the things I am working on and pursuing in this single part of my life.

Eternal Destiny

The most important thing to remember is that God wants you to progress, whatever your stage of life. Don't let Satan convince you that you can't progress while being single. It doesn't work like that. God is helping you become the best version of you, and one day you will rule kingdoms and worlds without number. All the things you are learning and working on will help you fulfil your eternal destiny to be a Goddess one day. Getting good at painting? That's got to come in handy for designing worlds one day. Everything you do for good is moving you along the right path. Even when life seems most difficult or unfulfilling, you can be taking steps toward your eternal destiny, which will be incredible. "What will it matter, dear sisters, what we suffered here if, in the end, those trials are the very things which qualify us for eternal life and exaltation in the kingdom of God with our Father and Savior?" (Linda S Reeves 'Worthy of Our Promised Blessings' Oct 2015). I feel the truth of that statement in my soul! It is all worth it.

Rachel A.'s Story

Growing up in the Church of Jesus Christ of Latter-day Saints, we hear about the temple constantly. "I love to see the temple, I'm going there someday…" And as a youth and young adult I attended regularly to participate in the ordinances of baptism and confirmation for the dead. I especially loved spending time in the temple in prayer and meditation and study. In the time, in the quiet, peaceful and reverent environment, it was natural for me to receive peace and comfort in times of struggle, gentle confirmations to decisions I was making and inspiration and instruction about my divine nature and the power of the Atonement of Jesus Christ.

I looked forward to the opportunity to attend the temple for my endowment one day and was actively preparing to do so. In a BYU religion course, our primary assignment was to ask a question about a gospel topic and then over the course of the semester we were to study and annotate any and all sources we could find in order to answer our own question. I asked, how do I best prepare to enter the temple? I received an A on the assignment which I share because I put hours into the assignment. I studied conference talks; lesson manuals; quotes from the prophets; books; the temple prep manual; many, many scriptures; and identified relevant material from each to understand the ordinances associated with attending the temple as well as what was suggested for me to be prepared to attend myself. I loved the assignment and was even more excited and hopeful for the point at which I would receive my endowment and participate in temple worship beyond the baptistry.

So, in 2011, after I graduated from BYU, before I started my Master's degree I decided that I wanted to go through the temple myself. The main thought for me was that I was approaching huge changes in my life, moving to a new city by myself, starting school to learn to be a therapist and I wanted the added blessings of my temple endowment to be with me as I started that journey. Beyond that, many of my friends had been married or were headed for missions and taking out their own endowments for those events, the boys I grew up with had been through the temple years earlier when they left on their own missions and my younger sister was herself getting married in the temple at the end of the summer, an event I didn't want to miss. Knowing all my peers were participating in temple ordinances didn't seem to be a reason to go myself but reassured me that I wasn't acting prematurely and increased my desire as they described their appreciation of the experience. I had prayed about my desire and felt confident and peaceful in my decision to pursue my endowment. I asked my Branch President for an appointment to discuss my intentions and we met together one evening.

We were at my home, not the Church building which I share because I can still so vividly picture sitting in my parent's living room with him for this discussion. I can feel the memory as if it was still happening because it was such a pivotal moment for me. I shared with the Branch President my desires and thought processes about being prepared to receive my endowment and instead of support and enthusiasm I was met with an answer of no. This man did not believe I was prepared and felt instead that it would be more appropriate for me to wait. He gave me two specific reasons. First, he wanted me to understand that once I made those covenants in the temple, I would be held to a higher standard in keeping those covenants. Of course, I understood this. But specifically, he wanted me to understand that for example if I was dating someone and messed up sexually with them, the consequences would be more severe should I make temple covenants of chastity. Therefore, it would be better for me to wait to make those covenants until after I was married so I wouldn't risk a sin in that way. Second, he believed that it would be more special if I shared my first temple experience with my future companion. He counseled me that I would be glad to have waited if instead of attending on my own, I went with my soon-to-be husband.

I was devastated. I wanted this so badly and to have been rejected outright felt painful. The experience left me questioning my own personal revelation since I'd felt so peaceful about my decision. My understanding of a leader's stewardship meant that I thought he could receive specific guidance for the situation that would trump my own and so I did not push back or question him; I simply let it stand, the answer was no. If I was faced with this situation today, understanding better that leaders are men with divine inspiration but not perfection, I would not
allow someone else to so quickly disregard something that I felt strongly about.

It would be dishonest if I didn't share that I am actually glad I did not receive my endowment that Summer. Had I attended the temple then, it would likely have been shared with my sister who was doing so in preparation for her marriage, and it would have invited so much opportunity for comparison, both with the actual experiences and with the circumstances of our attendance. By attending later, I was able to have a day that was mine and mine alone. I got to center my own experience of being there and was in a position to not have to worry about measuring up to her situation, which I did plenty of that summer without this particular event.

Despite that, I want to be clear that my Branch President's logic was wrong. If needed, I would still raise my hand and sustain him today as he was a kind, loving man who I know did his best in serving our branch. However, his reasonings for delaying my request seem to have missed a great deal of what is available in the temple. First, the questions and requirements of a temple recommend are the same both before and after you attend for your endowment. As I'd been living worthy of my recommend and attending the baptistry, there was no reason to assume that after receiving my endowment I would change my behavior. I had a great track record of being able to keep the law of chastity for example and had no intentions of altering that. Further, since I was typically dating Mormon men, many of whom had served missions, chances were that the future person I'd be dating would have already made his temple covenants. Why would it be acceptable for him to be "risking sexual sin" in this way but not me? Especially given that many youth lessons had suggested to me that women were the more responsible gender in such matters. The truth is that both before and after my endowment I have agency I am responsible to use carefully but a theoretical risk of consequence for sins I was not guilty of or prone to was not an appropriate reason to ask me to delay.

Second, the suggestion that the temple would be better if attended with my husband does not at all reflect the nature of the initiatory ordinances and the endowment. This message and others similar to it in our culture minimize the personal significance of the ordinances and covenants that one participates in for themselves in the temple. While there is a ritual associated with the endowment that is shared between spouses as part of the sealing ordinance, that is no reason for that to delay attendance initially. That ceremony is participated in on the day of one's sealing regardless of whether the endowment is occurring for the first or five hundredth time. If something is not true in both directions, it is a good red flag that there is something incorrect or incomplete about the idea. In this case my branch president suggested the temple would be more special if first attended with my spouse. However, again, it would be likely that my spouse would have attended before his mission. Would his experience not have been special? Or would later sharing it as spouses be lesser because of his previous attendance? Since we can answer of course not in both cases, we know it wouldn't be true in the other direction as well. The initiatory and endowment are beautiful and sacred individual ordinances and covenants.

    I continued holding a recommend and attending the baptistry until two years later when I felt prompted that I should ask again to receive my endowment. I was again facing changes about my future and felt I would greatly benefit from the additional learning available in the endowment. I was growing in painful but beautiful ways through all I was learning in my therapy degree and having a stronger connection to my spirituality was something I felt would help me continue. I also can describe perfectly where I was when I asked my Bishop for an appointment to meet with him. This time because the experience was so completely different from the previous one. We were outside at a park in Las Vegas in late June, the sun was setting but it was still warm. I asked if I could talk with him about maybe, possibly going through the temple and his reply was a joyful smile and supportive yes, of course, you can, I'd love to help you with that! I'd been so afraid to ask having been rejected so firmly before and all those fears were taken in a second.

My bishop was wonderful in encouraging and supporting me but unfortunately, I still had moments of struggle to feel like I deserved to be making this decision. The clearest example of this was when I went to the distribution center with my mother and sister to purchase my clothing in preparation for my day. We came in and said I was going for the first time and the woman working said "Marriage or Mission?!" When my reply was, "just for myself" her face almost fell and she simply replied, "oh." That entire experience of selecting my ceremonial robes was colored by her lack of response, which I interpreted as disapproval. I knew it didn't matter and that the experience was meant to be my own, but I couldn't help but think how she would have kept talking about the excitement of the other scenarios rather than ignoring mine.

The day of my endowment I felt SO nervous and when I walked into the temple and was assigned my worker she asked the same question, "Marriage or Mission?!" My heart sunk, did I really belong here if everyone felt there were only two reasons and I fit neither category? However, this time when I replied, "just for myself", she immediately beamed, hugged me and told me that was wonderful. "That reason is maybe even better" she whispered to me. She'll never know how much that mattered to how I experienced the rest of that day.

If I could sum up these experiences, I would have two lessons. First is on an individual level: your religious progression is your own. I chose to pursue my endowment without mission or marriage as part of mine but that doesn't mean that is the right version, just that it was the one I desired and felt assurance around. The choices you make in covenants and ritual should be the ones you feel personally inspired toward without pressure of culture or timeline. Even more important than that, your spiritual progression is your own. You have the right and privilege and opportunity and power and connection to personal revelation and you can trust those experiences. Advocate for yourself. Leaders are limited by what they know and can see and you get to articulate what you experience and believe and need as you interact with them. And most importantly, your relationship to Heavenly Parents and Jesus Christ is personal. They are loving, supporting, encouraging, guiding, praising, hoping for you individually.

The second is on a cultural level. We need to detach the idea that an endowment is something done only in preparation for mission or marriage. First, because it dismisses and damages those of us who are not participating for either of those reasons. And second, because it distracts from the beautiful nature of the ordinances and covenants themselves. When we link them we take away from all that is contained with that experience as being just a box to check before the bigger thing happens. In my experience, the initiatory and endowment were a big, beautiful day themselves and I would hate to think how they might have been overshadowed by the way we skip over them as just part of mission prep or a sealing day. We can do this better by shifting any beliefs that suggest single people are stunted or stalled on their journey to adulthood. Beliefs that say adulthood begins with marriage. For some those experiences will be interwoven but for many of us they occur separately.

Section 3
Relationships

"Christ taught that all of the gospel laws hang on our ability to love God and others (Matthew 22: 37-40). All of God's laws are ultimately laws of love. Every commandment is given out of love for you and concern for your happiness. Every commandment ultimately tests your ability to love Him and your fellowman" – Marleen Williams, "A Gospel of Relationships", *BYU Speeches*, May 2004

Chapter 7
Support And Boundaries

"As you learn to communicate openly, set appropriate boundaries and perhaps seek professional counseling. Maintaining spiritual health throughout the process is vital!" – Carole M. Stephens, "The Master Healer", *Ensign*, November 2016

Having a husband means having someone to lean on and support you. However even in the best marriages, most people still need support from others outside of their spouse, whether that is friends, family, or their ward. This can happen for any number of reasons. The point is that even when you are married you will need more people in your life than just your husband. As a single person, you have to rely on relationships outside of a marriage. Because of this, it is even more important that we know how to grow relationships and get the support we need.

But those relationships can bring challenges, too. People we love and who love us may say things that are hurtful, even when they are trying to help you. Learning to set proper boundaries and stand up for ourselves appropriately can help us not be hurt by others.

Things People Say

When I was in college, I sold tickets for the Utah Shakespeare Festival during the summer. It was a great job for a budding actress. I got to sit in the ticket office, talk to theater lovers, and dream of performing.

Most people call in advance to buy tickets, and then pick them up the night of the show. But as a long-standing theater with many long-time fans, we'd get people coming up in person to the window to buy tickets for shows in later months or even for the next year. Many of these were older women.

I enjoyed meeting these ladies. They would tell me about their favorite shows from past years, what they were looking forward to this year, and try to conceal their secret crushes for Brian Vaughn, one of the most popular actors who performs every year there.

Because they were nice, they'd often ask about me. Sometimes they'd ask if I was single. When I would say yes, they would light up and say, "Oh I bet you and my grandson would be just perfect together!" This happens all the time for me, but I have never had someone's son or grandson ever call. If I just had to impress the parents or family of a guy, I'd have been married 12 times by now at least. Once the mother of a guy I had a crush on told me, "If he ever grows up, I give you my permission to marry him!"

The point is, all single people, regardless of gender, religion, or anything else, have family trying to get them married.

Most of the time, these gestures from family come from a place of love. But it can be very stressful- at least that's how it was for me. I dealt with this for a while with my parents when I got back from my mission, especially with my mom. It got to the point where I felt anxious or upset at any mention of guys or dating. My parents are incredible and good people. I knew they wanted what's best for me, so for a while I just tried to suck it up.

What they didn't realize was that I was hurting and needed help. I couldn't just expect my mom and dad to realize that without me saying anything. With time I explained everything about how I was feeling, and how I felt when they said certain things. I told them about my anxiety and depression as well as my struggles with relationships. My parents met in high school and knew they wanted to get married at age 17. Since I was their oldest child and in a completely different situation, this was new territory for us all. I have learned I need to be as clear as possible and provide all the information I can so that they can assess the situation to best help me.

It's never going to be perfect. There are going to be well-intentioned people that say hurtful things all the time. That's just part of being human. But the more we can help change the dialogue around what we are experiencing, the better the world will be for it.

Family: Tell Them

Many times family and friends will say things like, "I just want to see you happy" when they try to give dating advice. Or when someone gets engaged, we write things like, "I'm so glad you found happiness!" on their Facebook announcement. What are the most liked social media posts? When a person puts that they are in a relationship. This always makes me roll my eyes- what if that guy is *terrible* for her? Why are we 'liking' a relationship we know nothing about? It's why there is so much pressure on relationships- because apparently that's how you become happy so you've got to hurry up and find someone to marry so you can be happy. This creates pressure and incorrect thoughts about marriage and leads a lot of people to *unhappiness*. It's not just married people I hear making these comments. I once had a roommate say it about her sister. She wanted to help her go on more dates and find "the one" *so she could be happy*.

I am not trying to say that I don't think marriage can add to happiness. But marriage isn't what automatically makes a person happy and being single doesn't automatically make a person unhappy. We can lift a lot of pressure from each other and find a lot of peace if we can let this go. The way to start changing this is to first notice if you are falling into this trap of linking happiness to marriage. Then, if you are bothered by something someone says, you can always say things like, "I always thought she seemed happy even before she got engaged". This will help bring awareness around the issue.

Relationships

A big challenge that many of the single women I have talked to face is not feeling like an adult in their family. They aren't expected to contribute to Sunday dinners because they are single. Or their picture on the mantle at their parents' house isn't updated from their high school graduation because the next picture is supposed to be the wedding picture. Talk to your family. They can't know what bugs you and hurts you if you don't bring it up. Don't wait for the feelings to boil up either. Calmly find a quiet time to talk one-on-one with your parents. I also had to talk to other members of my extended family because I couldn't deal with their advice about how to attract a husband.

If despite your best efforts, your communications with your parents don't go well and you're never able to get on the same page, don't despair. Parents are doing the best they can. I would invite you though, to learn to move forward, instead of feeling like the issues in your life are your parents' fault. You have the freedom to choose your life's path. Parents can help, but ultimately, it's your choice.

You can also help change the next generations. That's the power women have. When you do have an opportunity to counsel a daughter, or a niece, or a friend, instead of just preparing her for marriage, prepare her for herself. You might need to get professional help to overcome some family stuff. But it's worth it to fix you, because there will be many people that will depend on the wisdom you have gained from your life experiences. Never feel guilty about doing good for yourself!

Jealousy

Sometimes it's hard when you look around and see all the incredible things that everyone else is doing, especially if you feel the things you want aren't happening for you. One thing you can do is choose to be happy for others. Be happy for friends and roommates that *are* getting engaged and married. You might have

Support And Boundaries

to start out by forcing yourself to be happy. Smile! Take deep breaths and tell yourself that you truly are happy.

I have seen engaged girls downplay their happiness because they didn't want to hurt their best friend. The engaged girl is bursting with emotions she can't express with her best friend, so she hangs out with other people (especially her fiancé, who obviously is experiencing the same excitement). Be a good friend and be happy for her. Yes, you might still feel jealous. It doesn't mean you are a bad person for having those emotions. But deal with it in a healthy way. Acknowledge to yourself that you are jealous and that it's a temporary emotion. Then jump up and down with joy for your friend. Be happy for her. I promise you can feel real happiness for her. It's ok to cry too. But don't make your best friend feel miserable or guilty because of the good things happening to her.

Don't be surprised or hurt if your engaged friend has a hard time being there for you now. It's going to be tough, but you need to let her go. It's ok to talk about those feelings with your best friend, but be careful to avoid hurting her or bringing her down during this exciting time. If you need to express upset feelings more openly, talk to a different friend. I do think it's important to still have best friend time when you are engaged, and after marriage too. But be aware that her world is different now, and yours will be, too, one day. Learn from watching her take this step, instead of spending the time being miserable.

The thing that helps me the most when I feel jealousy is to think about my relationship with God. He loves me, and He is helping me have the best life I could possibly have and the one that will teach me the lessons I need to become a Goddess one day. This earth life is just a preparation for what is to come. As long as I am following God's plan, I've got amazing things in store now and in the future.

Being happy is a choice. In Alma 17, the angel comes to Ammon and his brethren and says "Be Comforted". And then it says, "And they were comforted." (verse 10) To me that has always meant that instead of murmuring and saying, "How can we be comforted? Do you realize what we are going through?!", they chose instead to allow themselves to be comforted by the spirit and be at peace despite current challenges and an unknown future. You can choose to be happy for other people and choose to be happy in your life. It is a choice. Choose to be comforted. Choose to smile even if you don't want to. It's not being dishonest or phony if you are trying. More often than not, I become happy because I try to be happy and that becomes authentic. But it can take a little work.

    I have heard women who are single say something along these lines: "If they can get married, why can't I?!" Might I suggest a different train of thought to use when you are feeling this way? Say instead to yourself: "If they are married, that gives me hope that I can be, too!" And remember again that marriage has nothing to do with intelligence, talent, or beauty. Make the most of the time you have and trust in God's plan for you.

<u>Friendship Boundaries</u>

    I have often discussed roommate friendship with my younger sister who is also single. We have talked about how important it is to recognize that no friendship will ever be exactly what you need from a marriage relationship. Sometimes we get really close to roommates (or friends) and it can fulfill us in many, many ways. However, it will never be the same as, or replace, a husband relationship. Make sure you set good expectations and boundaries for yourself as you deal with relationships. Don't expect a roommate to be more than a roommate, and don't try to be more than a roommate for someone else. Friendships are the best when we stay within the boundaries of that relationship.

Support And Boundaries

Surround Yourself With Goodness

We need relationships to help us thrive as human beings. That's why our hearts and bodies crave marriage. And yet I have found that when we aren't married, there is still a lot we can do to have great relationships and feel fulfilled.

Callings and Causes

One of the best ways I have found to make and grow friendships as well as overcome sad days, is to serve. There's a quote by Elder Renlund that I love. It talks about what to do when dealing with unfairness:

> When faced with unfairness, we can push ourselves away from God or we can be drawn toward Him for help and support...Rather than becoming bitter, let Him help you become better. Allow Him to help you persevere, to let your afflictions be "swallowed up in the joy of Christ". Join Him in His mission "to heal the brokenhearted", strive to mitigate unfairness, and become a stonecatcher.... All unfairness - especially infuriating unfairness- will be consecrated for your gain. (Elder Dale G. Renlund "Infuriating Unfairness" April 2021

His advice for overcoming unfairness includes healing and helping others. God has given us relationships with others so that we can serve them and get out of our own sadness some days. I have found that serving others is one of the best ways to get myself out of my own head.

One of the ways we can serve is in our wards. Ward callings can be fun. They can also be draining. At the very least they can be time-consuming. It can be tempting as a single person with all you need and want to do, to think you've got no time to really get into a church calling. I've definitely felt that way at times.

But other times I have really gotten into my callings. I did this once when I was called as ward choir director. It was a blast-so fun, in fact, that I decided to book us some gigs outside of church. One Christmas season, we went to several nursing homes and a hospital to perform. It was very unorthodox for a ward choir, I suppose, but it's the kind of thing I am used to doing with performing, and I loved it. I think it was really fun for the ward choir members too!

I share this because it really taught me that magnifying a calling can bring great personal fulfillment. I was able to use my talents and gifts which felt good. Just being able to serve also felt good. On top of that it was just fun to build relationships with ward members. I also had fun doing something not so traditional but within my wheelhouse of abilities, and it blessed even more people outside of our ward.

Another way to use service to grow relationships and build yourself is to join or create a cause. I love being part of groups that support overcoming pornography addictions, human trafficking, and resources for refugees. Those are causes that I personally connect with and have a passion for. If there are events I can attend, I love to participate. I always meet people that are passionate about that same thing, and this has blossomed into some fabulous friendships and relationships. It's usually not too hard to find things that you can passionately support. If a group doesn't exist near you for a cause you are interested in, consider creating your own. These kinds of groups bring people together with similar ideals and passions, so you meet a lot of great people and grow your circle of influence when you contribute to the community this way.

Grow your network

Years ago, one of my good friends at church was convinced we needed to be sisters. She wanted to set me up with one of her brothers, but I wasn't of the right age for any of them. After a while she realized that one of her brothers was close to the age of one of my sisters and she decided they needed to go on a date. They did, a few months later he proposed to her, and they have been happily married ever since. The moral of this story is that other people can be inspired to help you, so keep making relationships even if they aren't romantic.

Therapy

Working with a therapist is a relationship I didn't expect to have in life, but I am so grateful for it now. It taught me a lot about how to make healthy relationships with my fellow man and God as well. I learned about the power of thoughts, and their impact. The Atonement of Jesus Christ will heal us, but sometimes we don't even realize that we need to be healed, or what issues are weighing us down. That makes it hard to turn it over to Him. Yes, we have everything we need in the scriptures. But sometimes it's hard to pull out the things we need, because we don't know what we are looking for and we are still learning how to hear the spirit.

As I learned about the power of thoughts through my therapist, suddenly I started seeing examples all over the Book of Mormon of people who purposefully decided to have positive thoughts to help them. One example of this is Nephi, who after being tied up to the ship by his brothers said, "Nevertheless, I did look unto my God, and I did praise him all the day long; and I did not murmur against the Lord because of mine afflictions" (1 Ne 18:16). This is such good advice for people dealing with depression or anxiety- fill your life with gratitude towards God and don't look for ways to complain. I wasn't getting this out of the Book of Mormon on my own. It took meeting with someone who could look at my situation and talk to me about it before I was able to pull this truth from scripture. My relationships with others, including in my case a therapist, have helped me understand the scriptures better and how to overcome my challenges.

Relationships

Connecting With Others

If you're feeling lonely or sad, you're not the only one. When I am overwhelmed with loneliness, I try to remember that there are lots of people who feel lonely. Loneliness is a part of life, and it makes the non-lonely moments more valuable and precious. Getting support when you are lonely or sad is huge. Here are some ideas on how to do that:

Reach out

Reaching out to others, even in a small way, can make a big difference for you as well as the other person. So many people feel alone. When I feel lonely, if I just message someone to say hi, or try and do some ministering or something, I know I will feel better.

I had an enlightening conversation with a bishop once. He said that the people who come to his office and say they are lonely are people who do not go to ward activities, and usually only attend Sacrament Meeting. This taught me that it takes work to overcome the struggle of loneliness. It doesn't go away naturally. Like any hard thing in life, it takes effort to make it a strength. As we do the work, even when it takes us out of our comfort zones, it will help us and it will help people around us.

Serve

Another way to find yourself is to lose yourself. We learn that at church. Do acts of service. The feeling you get after you go visit someone is one of the best. I am not the best at ministering and a lot of times I just leave stuff on their doorsteps since I didn't coordinate a meeting, but I really feel great after.

Once my ward mission leader posted that he needed a sister to come with him to serve a sister who needed her kitchen organized and cleaned. I felt like I should do it, so even though it was last-minute, I went. I had been really struggling emotionally and mentally. I went and we started cleaning and talking to this lady, and suddenly I realized two hours had gone by! It felt great! I admit I like cleaning other people's houses, but I also think serving helps you forget about yourself. I did not think about my problems once, and even when I was done my issues seemed a little smaller. It was super nice. I lost two hours at work, but it was more than worth it to feel so much better. I am definitely gaining a strong testimony of service, and I'm learning that service is a blessing rather than a chore.

Get Help

It is also important to learn how to be served. In our culture, for some reason it seems nobler *not* to let others serve us unless something happens that is so bad, we have no choice. In her last talk as Relief Society General President, Sister Linda K. Burton counseled us to be "certain women"- meaning women who are convinced, positive, confident, firm, definite, assured, and dependable. Sister Burton talks about an amazing woman named Jenny, a Relief Society President who was diagnosed with leukemia. Sister Burton says, "Because Jenny is a Certain Woman herself, she invited all to share others' burdens, including her own".

A number of years ago my family went up to visit my grandparents. My grandma wasn't doing very well, so we were trying to visit as often as we could. During this particular visit, my sister Malorie was asking Grandpa questions. One of the questions was: "If you could go back and change one thing about your life, what would it be?"

He answered, "I'd have asked for more help along the way."

Of all the things my grandpa could have changed in his 80+ years of life, it would have been to ask for more help. He is an amazing man- he raised nine kids, served multiple missions, and benefited thousands of people throughout the world by his own service or that of his posterity. It's made me think of the scripture: "ask and ye shall receive. Knock and it shall be opened unto you". Perhaps the idea of asking for help is an important and eternal skill

Relationships

we are meant to develop in this life. God invites us to ask more, that the windows of heaven might be opened to us.

Not long ago, one of the sisters I ministered to asked me if I could walk her dog because she had sprained her ankle. I was so happy that she reached out to me! Ministering can seem so awkward and weird, but when someone actually reaches out, it reminds me what it's about! There's a purpose and I feel good when I can serve. I was thrilled she asked, and I felt like I developed a stronger connection to this sister.

One day I was bringing groceries in from my car. I had bought a bunch of pumpkins to decorate the front of my house with since it was October. As I was bringing in the first load, I passed by some roommates and friends in the living room. I could have kept going back and forth bringing in everything. But I remembered I was trying to get better at asking for help, so I did. They were happy to do it and that made me happy, too.

Asking for help can feel like a major risk. We might worry we will look weak or stupid. It can be very uncomfortable at first. However, I believe it is a very important skill to develop. My dad had the privilege of learning this important skill when he was a bishop in his mid-20's. He had people come in to talk to him and ask for help and guidance right when they needed it; others came in when it was too late. This taught him the importance of not waiting too long. He put that into practice when some tragic events hit our family. He could feel himself starting to go numb, so right away he went in to talk to the bishop. Although I don't know all the details of everything that happened, he has said it is what saved our family. Because he shared these experiences with me, I have learned to act on it as well.

It can be hard, but it is so much better to solve problems soon rather than letting things fester or holding it in until you explode. This happens to girls a lot. I know girls who are asked to do really hard things on their missions, for example. Their mission president doesn't realize what they are experiencing, because many times we think we 'should' be able to do anything we are asked to do. I have seen girls break down emotionally and leave the church because of this. If we understood the skill and importance of asking for help, as well as saying no when we have too much on our plate, this would be less likely to happen. Don't assume that someone will see your situation and save you from it, even a church leader. They are not perfect, and you get to learn to ask for help.

The way you learn to do this, is to start practicing asking for help *before* you think you really need help. While it might be more natural for most women to wait until they break to ask for help, that is not a good thing. It is not being strong or brave. It is not God's way. So, practice asking for help before you get to that point. If you feel like a calling might be too much to handle, talk to your bishop. Maybe you don't have to refuse it, but talk to him about your concerns. Perhaps you can get an assistant, or co-chair or something. At the very least if he knows how you are feeling about it, he can be sensitive. So many times whether we realize it or not, we expect men and leaders to be mind readers. They are not. If you are struggling, you are going to have to verbally communicate that in order to receive help.

One of the most important things you can ask for is a Priesthood blessing. I have seen many single women finally get the blessing they needed from one of the Elders Quorum members and it helps them so much! There is no need to wait until you are at the end of your rope to get a blessing. Take responsibility for knowing what you need and ask for a blessing. The Priesthood is always available to you as a member of the church. If the thought comes to you that you should get a blessing, DO IT!

Friends can be our Angels

When we don't have the blessings we want, God will compensate in other ways. I have been blessed in my life with family and friends that step in when I ask. Sometimes, it even happens when I don't ask.

I once had a call back for an audition coming up and needed to practice the music. I only had a couple hours between when I got the music, and when the audition would be. I was desperately looking for a place to practice. In my frantic searching, I got a knock on the door. It was a friend of mine. She said she felt like she should come over and ask if I needed help with anything. I sat there for a minute.

Then I asked, "Do you know where I can find a piano somewhere where I can practice in private?"

I was expecting her to say no. That seemed like quite the request. But she lit up and said, "Yes! My dad is a bishop and has keys to the church. Let's go!"

It wasn't the most important thing in the world, but in that moment, it was everything to me. I am so grateful for a friend that listened to the spirit. I am so grateful that God sends me angels when I need them. God does take care of us often through our relationships with others if we just look!

Relationships are crucial to human health and happiness. There are many important relationships outside of marriage. We single women can be a huge blessing to the Lord's work and others, in ways no one else can. The more we take care of ourselves through seeking support and setting proper boundaries, the more we can be used as instruments for good in the Lord's kingdom, as well as find personal peace and happiness.

Camilla C.'s Story

I used to tell myself I wanted to wait a while before I got married. Twenty-three would be a great age, I thought. How funny and naive that thought feels now.

Support And Boundaries

I grew up in a household where my mom was married at nineteen, her mother was married at twenty, and her mother's mother was married at eighteen. In my small bubble of a world, I didn't know anything different than young marriages with lots of kids to follow. I am the oldest of ten children, so for twenty-five years my mother was having children. My grandmother had five children with a couple miscarriages and unrealized dreams of having more children. My great grandmother had twelve children and her husband at ninety years old still jokes about wanting to have twelve more. I thought I had a very sophisticated and modern-day dream of waiting until twenty-three years of age to get married and having a modest amount of six children.

Unsurprisingly, given my expectations, twenty-four was a hard year for me. I imagine that somehow I'm not the only one who has faced this. We have a hard line of what we see for our lives, and suddenly, everything is not turning out as we thought it would. This was a pivotal year for me. It was the year when all jokes, comments, questions, and actions relating to my singleness became that much more annoying. It had gone from slightly uncomfortable to a painfully emotional reminder of what I deemed at that time as my failure in life.

I'm going to review a couple of those experiences, not to point out what was done wrong, but to point out what I learned from each of these experiences. I know none of these people meant any harm, and it could even be said these actions were done out of love, but we found an even better way to handle these situations. That allowed me to feel the love that I was intended to receive.

The first experience I had where I felt glaringly single and different was when my sister just younger than me was newly married. First, you have to know, my grandma is a master thrift store treasure hunter. She often claims that she can speak aloud what she is looking for and then it will show up at the thrift store the next time she goes. It's one of her talents and weaknesses. It becomes a weakness when you end up with too much of anything wonderful. In this case, she ended up with two too many of her favorite blenders, the Vitamix. In our family, it is a coveted kitchen tool because it's the only blender that can handle our hearty morning smoothies without burning out in a week. We were all very excited that we might receive the extra blenders that my grandma had found. The next time I saw my grandma, she was mentioning her plans for the blenders. One would go to my sister and her new husband, since they were married. The other one would go to either my cousin and her new husband, or she said she thought she might hold on to it for me until I got married. I remember being shocked and hurt enough that I couldn't even stand up for myself at that time. In my mind I had just been told, "You are not a real adult, a whole person, until you are married." I remember the lump in the back of my throat preventing me from speaking. My grandma loved me so much. I knew that. But why did she think I was not complete? The sarcastic side of my brain thought, "A single person would never want to make a smoothie. Only a married person would do such a thing." I don't remember if I ever addressed this issue with my grandma, or if she came to her senses on her own; all I know is today I am the proud owner of a thrift shop Vitamix.

    Even more profound, I learned some valuable lessons after experiences that prompted some very troublesome questions. Why am I here on earth? Can I be happy without being married? Should I continue pressing forward if I'm just to remain single? Was I actually not whole? On the surface, I thought I knew these questions, but I didn't know them in my heart. I still have days that I call my "Sad Single Days". But now I also know I'm not just born here to be someone's wife and bear children. I greatly hope to experience both of those things, but I am here on earth because I am a child of God and I want to become like him. I don't have to be married for that. I now know if I'm not happy on my own, I can never be expected to be happy in a marriage. Now I know I should keep pressing forward because I can still progress, serve, and fulfill

Support And Boundaries

a purpose. Most importantly, I am whole as I rely on the Atonement of Christ. He is the only thing that completes us.

I was recently talking to a friend who got married very quickly and later got divorced. He said, "I didn't need a marriage--I needed a therapist." Marriage is not the avenue that completes us, and now that I know that deeply, I am happier and ready to communicate that to my own loved ones.

The second and last experience I will share was with my immediate family. I had come home just as everyone was kneeling down for family prayer, so they invited me to kneel in a circle with them. One of my siblings who was probably pre-teen age was saying the prayer. As we often do, they were going through all of the siblings and praying for them individually with a specific blessing they needed. Yes, that can take quite a while with ten children. When the prayer got to my name, they said "Bless that Camilla will find a man to take her to the temple." I remember being so embarrassed. I wasn't living at home at the time, so I was just imagining that this was a prayer that was often said while I was away. The somewhat innocent pre-teen was just regurgitating a prayer that he or she had heard prayed before probably many times. Without a doubt, it came from a place of love. But again, my mind heard, "Camilla, you can't go to the temple on your own. And you are so incomplete without a husband, that your whole family prays for this while you are away, and even more humiliatingly, in your presence."

Thankfully, I had learned a lot about communication since the blender incident. I also learned this was not my shame to carry. There is nothing shameful about singleness. Even though it was hard, I did talk to both of my parents about what their well-intentioned prayer made me feel. I asked them to set the example in changing how they approached my situation because their attitude was influencing my siblings. I set clear boundaries about what I was okay with, and what would help me feel valued when I was at home. I wanted home and family to be a safe space. Now I can say that it definitely is, but that did not come without

Relationships

vulnerability, communication, and work. My family was oblivious to my hurt, so I had to say something, and I'm grateful for my family members who were humble and caring enough to change their actions. Boundaries, boundaries, boundaries! It's what has saved my relationship with my family in many instances, but especially in situations related to singleness.

Chapter 8
Connecting With God

"So, in the midst of this refiner's fire, rather than get angry with God, get close to God." Elder D. Todd Christofferson, "Our Relationship with God," *Ensign,* May 2022

Grow Closer To God

It is very important to have a great relationship with God before getting married. According to an article by Stephen Cranney in *BYU Studies Quarterly* ("Who Is Leaving the Church?: Demographic Predictors of Ex-Latter-day Saint Status in the Pew Religious Landscape Survey", 58:1, 99-108) , a divorced person has a 70% chance of leaving the Church. In a church that is very focused on marriage and family, a person who is single or divorced can feel isolated and even ostracized. It makes me wonder if perhaps our testimony can be in the culture and personal expectations more than in God and the Gospel of Jesus Christ. Whatever we can do now to be centered on the right things for our testimony, and grow a relationship with God, will help us no matter what comes our way.

Mostly I want to talk next about how to grow closer to God during this specific time of your life. But first, I want to recognize that sometimes there are specific difficulties with growing close to God that come from being single in a church where family is everything. If you have felt this, you are not alone. Sometimes trials, including being single, can put your relationship with God on the rocks.

I grew up always wanting to be close to God. I wasn't necessarily good at that, but I never had a reason not to want to be close to him, even when my family went through some pretty terrible things.

Relationships

When I was around 24, I had an experience that rocked this foundation of faith in God. I received an extremely strong impression that a certain guy was to be my husband. It was the strongest revelation I had ever received, and so clear I had a hard time trying to pretend it was anything but revelation. I was very surprised by this. For one- even though I had been talking almost daily to this young man for close to 2 years, we weren't dating. The biggest reason for that: we lived on the other side of the world from each other. We had only known each other in person on the mission. I had often prayed for help to get over him, so that I could date guys around me. But somehow, I would end up talking to "Mr. Out-of-the-country" again.

Well, I wasn't sure what to do about this information. Just hold on to it, I thought. But I needed to tell someone. I told my parents. They were surprised, but then they both prayed about it. They came to me a few days later and said they both felt like it was right. My dad told me that I needed to buy a plane ticket and go there as soon as possible. I was very nervous to do this, but I agreed.

After I bought the plane ticket, I told my friend I was going. It had been all fun and games for him up until this point. Now it scared him to the point where he almost vomited. But I had the ticket, and I was going. I asked him if I could stay at his sister's house, and he helped me make the plans.

Two weeks later, I showed up in a country I had never been to. I felt like I was going to be sick as well. I thought things would get better when I saw him; they didn't. We were both as stiff as boards. I was there for about 10 days, and they were traumatic. He barely said a word to me the whole time. He seemed to not even want to get physically close to me, let alone emotionally or romantically. I was humiliated, and so incredibly relieved to get on the plane home.

As I was heading home, I got upset. Why would God do this to me? Why would He tell me I was to marry a guy only to lead me on an expensive, embarrassing, terrible trip? I even felt like perhaps God was trying to play a joke on me or humiliate me.

I couldn't shake that feeling, for years actually. I never stopped praying or reading my scriptures or going to church and all the regular things. But I was crushed. I felt so let down by God.

Sometimes God gives us hard, lonely experiences so that we learn to go to Him. In an article entitled "Enduring Well" by Neal A Maxwell, from the April 1997 *Ensign*, it says: "...Part of enduring well consists of being meek enough, amid our suffering, to learn from our relevant experiences. Rather than simply passing through these things, they must pass through us... in ways which sanctify (us)." Your relationship with God can become so much stronger during this single time. Focus on sanctification, rather than self-pity or doubt. When you are close to God, you will get to know His voice.

Healing eventually came. The biggest thing that helped was looking for the good in the situation. Perhaps God wanted me to prove to myself that I do put God first in my life, that even when it is terrifying and embarrassing and painful, I will do what the Lord asks me to do. He is my number one source of strength and guidance. Would I go through that experience again if God asked me to? Yes, I would. Telling myself this strengthened me. I really did love God more than my fears of embarrassment and pain.

I was also able to learn a lot from this experience about relationships. I learned that pressure is debilitating in a relationship. I had naively given myself and my friend 10 days to try and fall in love. On top of that I was uncomfortable trying to learn his culture, language, and meet his entire family during those same 10 days. That kind of pressure made me extremely tense, and it was hard to have any kind of natural romance.

There were other things I learned as well. It was my first international flight alone, which built my confidence for more travel. I also learned a lot about revelation, and that sometimes what you hear in revelation is supposed to get you to take the next step in your life to learn and grow, not necessarily create the results you think it will.

All in all, though there were some hard years dealing with that experience, I can now say that I am grateful to the Lord and closer to Him because of it. I also understand more about how He works, and it has helped me trust Him more.

Put Christ first

Christ is really good at being a best friend. You can't have a better best friend than Him. In fact, he is perfect at it!
Elder Oaks shared the following experience on his Facebook page on July 11th, 2016:

> I received a letter from a woman studying at Harvard University. I was impressed with its content.
>
> She said, "I am only 26 and I have felt the trial of singleness overtake me."
>
> After sharing more in her letter, she concluded: "I was walking home from work one afternoon one year ago, pouring my heart out to God, telling Him my deepest desire was to be a wife and mother. I was stopped in my tracks as a powerful thought and feeling came into my heart and mind. The thought was that I was wrong. The deepest desire of my heart should be discipleship of Jesus Christ and then the second can be to be a wife and mother. My outlook on life has changed since then. I had them switched around. I know all the blessings promised will be mine, but this will happen in the Lord's time and not mine." What a powerful thought!

> Elder Neal A. Maxwell taught, "Since faith in the timing of the Lord may be tried, let us learn to say not only, 'Thy will be done,' but patiently also, 'Thy timing be done.'" We may say, "Thy will be done," but when your heart is aching - perhaps you're not yet married and you desire to be - it would be wise to also say, "Thy timing be done." Ask the Lord for continued revelation to guide your life.
>
> The Lord has His own timetable for His children. In life's experiences, including marriage, parenthood, and many other things, each timetable will be different. We must have faith and trust in the Lord to know that He is there and that He loves us. All promised blessings will one day be yours.

This article really helped me put things in perspective. It may be a blessing to be single while learning this lesson of putting God first- what easier time than when it is just you and Him?

No matter how hard things are, remember God won't do something to you that isn't for your benefit! He says so in 2 Nephi 2:24 "He doeth not anything save it be for the benefit of the world; for he loveth the world, even that he layeth down his own life…" Just because you get married doesn't mean you are going to magically always be held during your hard times. Find family members or good friends who can help and support you. Figure out what relying on God feels like, and how to get peace from Him regardless of your current situation.

I have struggled at times with knowing how to apply the Atonement of Jesus Christ to my life. It works differently for everyone, based upon how the spirit talks to you.

Relationships

Here's something that helps me though. I learned this 'trick' from my mom. Picture yourself walking in a garden or some peaceful place. Christ is there, and you walk up to him. Then you hand him your trial, or pain, or whatever is troubling you. He takes it from you and now you no longer carry it. This has been helpful with dating relationships (I imagine a specific guy being miniature so I can pull him out of my pocket and put him in Christ's hands).

I invite you to study the Atonement of Jesus Christ and figure out how it works for you. It's a lifelong process to really nail it, so don't expect yourself to be perfect at it. If you get 1% better at coming unto Christ every year, you'll be quite successful over a life time. And one of the biggest benefits is when you trust Christ, it's easier to trust His timing.

Journal

Something else you can do to build your relationship with God is write a journal. I started writing a journal when I was about six years old. I have not always been consistent, but it is so cool and enlightening to be able to go back and read over things from my past. Journaling is one of the ways that I sort through emotions, and this has helped me with my relationship with God and my relationships with others. Sometimes I'm not sure why I'm upset or sad, but as I start writing about it, answers come.

I also started a prayer journal. This is where I write a letter to God, and invite him to respond to me through my pen. It has been a really good exercise for me to learn how to better hear God and seek and receive revelation. Sometimes it's hard to tell what's me and what's God, but Moroni 7:12 says, "...all things which are good cometh of God..." Keeping that in mind keeps me on track. Then as I see things fulfilled, it builds my confidence and trust in this process.

Connecting With God

Let God Prevail

One of my greatest challenges in life is understanding control. I want to let God be in charge of my life. I want to be an easy going, carefree kind of person. I might already appear that way to a lot of people, because I am good at having fun. But that is different than being free of care. Instead of being able to turn my cares over to God and trust that everything is going to be ok, I try to *make* things be my way and be ok.

I sometimes confuse this with the importance of being proactive. In Elder Bednar's CES Broadcast in 2006 entitled "Seek Learning By Faith" he says: "endowed with agency, we are agents, and we primarily are to act and not only to be acted upon…" I sometimes think that means I have to be constantly busy doing something. I'm trying not to just sit around and wait for God to give me all the answers; I'm being proactive. But, here's the thing. Sometimes being an agent means learning to actively be patient. Learn *how* to wait. We need to do things on God's timetable, rather than force them to happen on ours. Sometimes we have to learn that we should not run faster than we have strength (Mosiah 4:27). God never tells us we need to be Superwoman.

I started learning the importance of not trying to be Superwoman on my mission, from my mission mom (wife of the president of the mission). Near the end of my mission, everything was stressing me out and I never felt like I was doing enough.

The last two transfers of my mission I was in a town called Yacuiba near the border of Bolivia and Argentina. I was one of two sisters starting out training that transfer. Unfortunately, on the first day, the other training sister broke her ankle. This meant that I was training two new sisters and taking care of a sister who was in physical pain and who was frustrated because she couldn't work. I was also trying to take care of the other sister missionaries in our village (I was the only sister training leader of my mission) while preparing six people for baptism in one area, and opening another area. In my mission, someone was paid to make our lunches, and

Relationships

since the sister with the broken ankle couldn't leave the house, we had to bring her lunch every day. After picking up the lunch, we had to walk over a mile to the house, carrying the meal in heavy pots and pans. If that wasn't enough, of the two sisters I was training, one didn't speak the language, and one was too scared and depressed to want to try teaching. I was entering my last transfer (six weeks) and trying not to be homesick. It was the hottest time of the year- we were dealing with 105-115 degree weather each day. In the night it got so hot sometimes that the electricity gave out and our fans stopped. I would instantly wake up when this happened, mostly because my bed would be soaked in sweat in about 20 seconds. The water for the shower didn't last long- it would trickle a small stream of water that allowed us each to take a two- minute shower. Christmas was coming up. I was battling my own depression and anxiety. I was miserable.

One day, it became too much. I just couldn't leave the house, which made me feel so guilty I wanted to die. I had only a few more weeks before I would be going home. I had already called my Mission President's wife a couple weeks prior about the stress, and I felt like I would be a total annoyance if I called again. But I couldn't go on, so I called her. She told me that of course it was ok that I called her. Then, she told me a story that I knew, but applied it in a way that changed my life.

She told me the story of Vincenzo Di Francesca, whose story is documented in the short film *How Rare a Possession*. In his search for truth, he was led to find a Book of Mormon sitting on top of a trash can and he was converted to the gospel and baptized after a long waiting period. After sharing this story, she emphasized that God used a trash can to convert one of His children to His gospel.

She asked, "Does God *need* you to accomplish His work, or could He do it on His own if He wanted?"

"He could give the gospel to the world without me," I answered.

"Well then," she said, "quit trying to be more than a trash can! God does not tell us to be Superwoman. If He can use a trash can to do His work, then you are certainly enough to do His work."

This conversation changed my heart. My best efforts were and are enough. And my best effort does not mean overdoing it. It means doing the best I can keeping myself above, not under water. If I am so stressed I can't think, how can I do what really matters?

After talking to my Mission President's wife, I gave myself permission to take a break. Even though the first companion I was to take out that day was ready, I told her I needed some time first to mentally prepare. I was worried it would take me a long time to get to the point where I could go outside. But it didn't even take an hour. Just giving myself the freedom to say that I need a break did wonders for my mental health. I was able to go out that day and had a very productive day, because I took the time to be ready for it. I would not have been as productive if I would have just kept pushing through all the stress and frustration I was holding on to.

The next day, as I was pouring cereal into my bowl for breakfast, the toy in the cereal fell into my bowl. Guess what? It was a Superwoman action figure. I laughed. To me, it was God saying that He knew exactly where I was and what I was doing, and that he agreed with my "Mission Mom". Taking breaks is a part of His plan. I'm not perfect at balancing stress and breaks. Sometimes I still don't break enough, and sometimes I break too much. But life is about learning and every time I evaluate and try again, I'm winning.

Liken The Scriptures

Another way I have grown closer to God is by reading the scriptures. The individuals in the stories are incredible people, and wonderful examples. As I find ways to connect to scripture characters, their stories become not only real to me, but I relate. I realize I'm not the only one who has had to go through hard things. The more I read the scriptures, the more people I have to relate to. It's so great! During different times in my life, Noah, Nephi, Oliver Cowdery, and more have felt like my best friends, because I felt like I could relate to them in so many ways. Sometimes this connection hits me as I read the scriptures. Something about their story would stand out to me, and I'd think, "that's just like me!" Other times, I have been in a situation, or something happens, and then a story from the Bible or Book of Mormon comes to my mind that brings me peace or understanding.

Abraham is definitely one of my scripture friends. I bond with him because I feel like I've been waiting to find my future husband for *forever*, but Abraham actually did wait 100 years before he had a son. As I have studied his story in depth, I feel such a connection and love towards him. So many of the things he went through are similar to things I have gone through. Obviously, those experiences were on a different level, but the spirit helps me to see the connections, and I feel blessed to have my scripture friends with me when I need them.

Abraham's wife Sarah is also amazing. One of my favorite scriptures is Genesis 21:12. In this verse God tells Abraham to listen to Sarah. Sometimes it's easy to find sexism in the scriptures, because of the imperfections of man. But God really does love His daughters as much as He loves His sons, and this is clear in the scriptures if you look for it. Sarah couldn't have children, which probably made her friends, family, and neighbors think she was being punished by God. She could easily have felt abandoned by God and turned away from Him. Instead, she tried to do what's right, and made sacrifices to move the work of the Lord along despite the trials that seemed unfair and undeserved.

Mistakes Are Part Of His Plan

Making mistakes is an important part of eternal progress. It was Satan's plan to make life a time that allowed no sin or mistakes. I have learned to be grateful for mistakes, through working with my dad.

Working in business with my dad has been a humongous blessing in my life. If it weren't for him, I wouldn't have been able to survive in business. During the first two years at my job, I would constantly go through the entire box of tissues in his office on a regular basis. Figuring out how to do the work meant such a huge learning curve. He would let me cry and cry, but over time, he allowed it less and less. At first I was hurt and felt ignored. But it forced me to figure out and try things out on my own. He was still always there, but instead of doing everything for me like I usually wanted him to, he kept stepping back more and more to allow me to learn and try and progress.

There were days when I would make mistakes and lose a client, and I would be mad at my dad because I knew it wouldn't have happened if he would have been with me. Because he didn't step in and save me all the time, I have been able to learn and develop skills on my own, and I am much more competent and able than I would have been without those lessons. What a gift he gave me!

I feel like God works in the same way. He is always there, but He doesn't step in and solve everything for us, because He is more concerned about us learning to be like Him, than in us never making a mistake. This helps me when I wish God would just do everything for me and make things work out perfectly.

One of my favorite songs is "Just Be Held" by Casting Crowns. My favorite lines says something like: your world is not falling apart, it is falling into place. Things like losing a loved one, making mistakes, or not having life turn out as we expected are painful and make you feel like your life is falling apart. The beauty of the Gospel of Jesus Christ is that all things are made right through Christ, and that any story can be rewritten for good when we turn these things to Him. He takes things that seem to be falling apart and makes them fall into place perfectly for us. We can't mess up God's plan; He is the ultimate rewriter.

Relationships

<u>Still Obey</u>

It can be so hard being single so long, and the years just keep going by, and it seems God has lost track of you. When I have days like that, I turn to a quote I love from The Screwtape Letters by C.S. Lewis. It reads:

> "(Satan's) cause is never more in danger than when (we), no longer desiring, but still intending to do (God's) will, look round upon a universe from which every trace of Him seems to have vanished, ask why (we) have been forsaken, and still obeys."

It is hard. But I did not come to the world to have an easy ride. I came here to learn how to be like God, and grow my relationship with him through my Savior, Jesus Christ. It might never go the way I hope, but I am learning and growing my faith that His ways are higher than my ways, and that His plan is better than my plan. I am growing closer to Him, and that makes everything I go through in life worth it.

<u>Natalie O.'s Story</u>

Growing up, I always thought I'd be married by 23 at the latest. I'm a pretty social being, and never had a shortage of guys to date. Life was all planned out: high school, college, mission, get married, have kids, live happily ever after. That was all I wanted out of life, and never did I think that would be too much to ask.

I got a year's worth of college credit in high school and finished my bachelor's degree three years later, at the age of 21. I left for a mission two months after graduation. My mission was the best experience of my life. I came back a month before my 23rd birthday; all was going according to plan.

Then I waited patiently for the next step to happen. As time went on and Mr. Right kept eluding me, I'd simply pick something to "tide me over" until I found him. First, it was teaching at the MTC. Then I went back to school for a master's degree. (When people asked why I was getting a graduate degree, I literally told them, "Just needed a next step in life.") I took a couple trips to Europe and Thailand. I landed a job at an advertising agency that was SO fun.

A year into that job, things started going wrong, and eventually it came to a traumatic end. And that's when I realized I was nothing but a floater – a substance-less piece of cotton from an aspen tree that settles momentarily on a bush, then a rock, then a weed, only to be swept up by the next gust of wind, never truly finding a place to land.

At this point, you're probably thinking, "This girl obviously needs to discover her identity as an individual, instead of putting all her hopes in a foolish fairytale and withering away until a man makes her 'complete.'" Because that's exactly what I thought, and the attitude I took on. I decided I was going to find my purpose in life because being a wife and a mom might never happen. I decided that I should learn how to be happy without it, that I should keep progressing. I prayed and fasted and got blessings, searching out the thing that God "meant" for me to do. I eventually settled on the idea of going back to school for Ph.D. and becoming a college professor. Things were looking up again.

But deep down... I was lying. I could fake the independent-successful-happy-woman attitude, but I didn't mean it, and I certainly didn't feel it. The thought of going back to school literally made me want to vomit. I was sick of making decisions based on "shoulds" instead of "wants." I was sick of feeling like society (especially the younger generation) was setting a precedent for me: that desirable, respectable human beings are those that climb corporate ladders and contribute to society and have a passion for some movement or idea or endeavor.

Well GUESS WHAT? I don't. I don't have a passion that I want to turn into a career. I don't have one thing that I feel is my purpose. I have a job that puts a roof over my head and food in my stomach and allows me to add to my shoe collection when I feel like it. And here's what I've learned:

1. It's okay to want good things. You don't have to bury your desire to be a wife and a mom, and you don't have to cover it by being some bad-ass business woman or scholar or [fill in the blank]. It's also okay to be sad that you don't have what you want. Christ is sad with you.

2. People usually have many purposes in life, not just one. For a few years, my purpose was to be a student. For some other years, my purpose was to serve in Relief Society. And not only can purposes be short-term, but one can be serving multiple small purposes at the same time. For example, one of my purposes right now is to be a good roommate and friend to a girl that depends on me for support and interaction. In fact, I don't even like the word "purpose"; being her friend isn't something I do purposefully – it's just who I am. We're told all the time that before we came to Earth, we were predestined for something great. Well, that something great is the conglomerate of all the teeny tiny good things you do in your life, the effect of who you just ARE. Which brings me to my next point…

3. You have worth because you exist. I'd heard that before, but I don't think I understood what it really meant. I would think, yes, my existence is tied to my family and others who love me. I have skills and abilities as part of who I am, and therefore I can affect others with them. NO. I mean this: God made you, and he loves you because he made you. Think of some little craft or object that you created… for me, it's a plate that I painted at Color-Me-Mine that is just so dang cute and I'm so proud of it every time I look at it. It isn't just worth something because I could trade it for

something else of value, or because it serves the purpose of holding my food. It simply brings me joy because it exists, and I made it.

I don't have everything figured out. I'm still dealing with depression and anxiety and seemingly meaningless days. But I don't have anything to be TRULY unhappy about. Christ really does and will make up for everything, and the older I get as a single woman, the more that phrase genuinely supports my soul.

Chapter 9
Church Culture

"Come, help us build and strengthen a culture of healing, kindness, and mercy toward all of God's children." Elder Dieter F. Uchtdorf, "Believe, Love, Do," *Liahona*, November, 2018

As members of the Church we tend to think that pressure to marry young is only found in the church. However, in my experience the difference seems to be that we get *married* sooner- we aren't single longer. Dating and engagement periods are longer outside of church culture, but people still want to be in a relationship, and for many people it seems that younger is better.

For example, one time I was waiting in line at the Walmart checkout behind two girls that seemed to be about college age. Because of their language, dress, and what they were talking about, I assumed they were not members of the Church of Jesus Christ of Latter-day Saints. As they got to the cash register, they started up a conversation and I listened. In the 10 minutes it took to check out (it took longer than usual because of the conversation), I learned that the cashier was 17 and in love with her boyfriend who would be proposing to her any day. The girls checking out were 19 and 20 and were jealous because they were *so* old and didn't even have boyfriends. They said they felt like they were falling behind and that it must be that the 17-year-old was so pretty- that's why she was in a relationship.

At first, 29-year-old me stood in line behind them wishing they would hurry up because it was Friday night and I wanted to get back to the TV show I was watching. (Friday night is a great time to go shopping by the way- there are less people than Saturday, that's for sure. And the dress code is pajamas.) But it was another reminder that culture outside of religion is pushing early relationships, too. I mean come on, have you seen Disney's *High*

School Musical? Or what about Disney's *Descendants*? (I watched that one with my 11-year-old sister recently- the main characters get engaged at age 17! They are in high school!) There are a *lot* of movies about people falling in love in their early 20s or even before. So Hollywood is affecting us, too.

What It Looks Like

Most of the issues I have heard people express about church culture impact married and unmarried people alike. There are a few specifics for singles.

Things that are said

I read an *Ensign* article on the Church website by Sister Kathleen Lubeck called "Singles and Marrieds" that talked about things that impact singles that can be called the culture of the church. It was written in April 1987, and a lot is very applicable to today. In the article, Sister Marie Cornwall, a BYU sociology professor, discusses how important it is to be sensitive in the way we talk to single people.

> Almost inevitably, single people are asked in a good-natured way, "Why isn't a beautiful woman (or handsome man) like you married?" The question implies that being single is not acceptable, says Sister Cornwall. "Just as couples who have been unable to have children appreciate the sensitivity of others who do not pressure them as to why, single members appreciate the sensitivity of others who do not pressure them about their singleness."

I saw a similar idea come up in a sacrament meeting not too long ago. When I was a foster mom for a year, I went to a family ward more, so that my teenager could participate in the young women's group and get to know the people in the ward. The area where I live tends to have a lot of newly married couples that move in and out. One Sunday a new couple was introducing themselves and giving talks. The wife, who was very pregnant, got up first. One of the things she said was: "I used to think that getting married was winning. Now I know it is just the beginning".

Both of these sentences are revealing and harmful in our thought process as a culture. The first sentence might be the one more obvious to most people- if we think of marriage as the destination, reaching that goal can sometimes cloud judgement in marrying the right kind of partner.

But the second sentence is just as bad, and I think a lot of people don't realize it. The girl making the statement certainly didn't- she seemed to think she had a mature realization. However, this is why people are constantly pushing older single adults to get married, even if it isn't to a good companion. It's because they truly believe you won't be happy, and your life doesn't *begin*, until you are married. This is so damaging to our aging group of singles- does it mean that all this unmarried time is a waste? Pointless? Good for nothing? And when ward members treat us like singleness is a waste of time or leaders don't ask us to serve, it's hard not to make that conclusion.

Another issue that Sister Cornwall brings up, is that married people don't think that single people have as much to do as them. She writes:

> "Married persons often think that singles have few responsibilities and lead simple lives," says Sister Cornwall. This is usually not the case. "Because there is no partner to share in the task of daily living, the single person must do everything— laundry, yardwork, shopping, painting, laying sod, automobile repairs, waiting for the repairman to come, earning a living. Doing everything is difficult, particularly so for the single person with children."

For me, even just reading that last quote helped me feel validated. Sometimes I feel like I should be doing more with my life because I don't have kids. But really when you understand that you are doing the work that two people usually do, even without children (obviously a huge piece), it is quite a lot! When you add dating (which can be equivalent to a part-time job), it is no wonder we feel overwhelmed sometimes.

Communicate Needs

When it comes to church culture, there are a couple of common negative behaviors some of us have. These behaviors often start with good intentions, like not wanting to hurt someone else's feelings. However, they can be taken too far, and cause problems with roommates or a future spouse.

Passive-aggressive

The first issue I will address is Passive-aggressive behavior. It is defined as: "… a type of behavior or personality characterized by indirect resistance to the demands of others and an avoidance of direct confrontation, as in procrastinating, pouting, or misplacing important materials" (Google dictionary).

When I was a Resident Assistant during my senior year of college at Southern Utah University, I learned that it is a behavior especially common in female members of our Church. I thought that was rather unfair for my bosses (who were not members of the Church) to say. But now with over 10 years' experience of living with roommates, I can say it does come up a lot.

This behavior can be seen in a number of ways. You might be doing it and not realizing it. If you leave sticky notes around the house with your requests instead of talking to your roommates, that is passive-aggressive. If you are really happy around your roommate but then send a text to them right after you leave for Christmas break listing your complaints, that is passive-aggressive. Giving someone the silent treatment is another example, or one of my favorites: I had a roommate who would make a mess of the silverware when she put it away to alert me that she was upset with me.

I believe that our church culture sometimes breeds passive-aggressive behavior because we are trying to be good and kind like Jesus, but we aren't sure how to talk about the hard things and be nice at the same time. Because we are afraid of a fight or confrontation happening, we avoid direct communication. We feel we aren't loving one another when we bring up something that might hurt their feelings.

We have it drilled into our minds to be nice, but we don't always learn that sticking up for our needs or disagreements *can* be nice.

Some women grow up watching their parents be passive-aggressive, so it's hard to know how to *not* be that way. If you see yourself struggling with this, here are a couple of tips:

1. Practice labeling your emotions. You might not really know what you are experiencing and feeling, so perhaps journalling your thoughts will help.
2. Work on understanding your worth and value. Your voice deserves to be heard, and your needs are important.
3. Remind yourself that sticking up for your needs and talking about concerns are good things. You are not a bad person for doing these things.
4. Ask your roommate how they would like to talk about hard things when they come up. (They come up for everyone! It's normal.)
5. If you have a lot of trust with a roommate, ask them to tell you if they think you are being passive-aggressive so you can start to notice it.

If you are struggling because you have a roommate that is passive-aggressive, here are some pointers for you:

1. Take deep breaths. Be grateful that you have learned healthy communication skills.

2. Without being judgmental, you can ask about the behavior (example: I notice you slammed your water bottle on the table before storming out of the room. Is there something bothering you? Make sure you practice your tone of voice in advance.)
3. Let them know that you see something is wrong, but that you do not know what the issue is. You would like to help with the concern, as soon as they are ready to talk about it, but that there isn't much you can do until they talk to you.
4. If you get a text of complaints, let them know you are sorry they have been bottling this all up, and you'd be happy to talk to them about it when they get back from work or back in town, etc. (Recognize that this was probably extremely hard for them to do, and they are more scared of you than you are of them.)
5. Show them love and work on being a safe person that they feel comfortable talking to.

Bottling

Bottling is what I call it when I suppress an emotion, and then it explodes out. I have seen it in myself when I think that instead of addressing the issue, I should just suck it up because that's the nice thing to do. This behavior often starts with good intentions. Your roommate does something that annoys you. Maybe she never changes the toilet paper roll when it runs out. You don't want to confront her about this, because you are trying to be Christlike. You tell yourself "It's not that big of a deal" and it's probably your fault for being annoyed. You want to just forgive and move on, but it's not working. And the problem is, it's not going away. You are trying so hard to let it go, but it's just getting worse. Sometimes, this leads to an explosion when you least expect it, and you might end up attacking your roommate over something trivial.

Don't worry! You can overcome this. No one - not a single friend, family member, or future husband, will ever be able to read your mind. You can learn how to appropriately talk about what is bothering you, and people won't be upset. No, not everyone is going to conform to your habits or beliefs. And they shouldn't. But you do need to bring up things that are upsetting you, especially if it's causing you stress and/or anxiety. A lot of people struggle with confrontation, which is normal. When you practice being rational and kind and talking about a situation before it reaches a crisis, confrontation can lose its negativity. The discussions that result can help build relationships and strengthen a home. If this is one of your weaknesses, remember that God will make weak things become strong if you let Him (see Ether 12:27).

Here are some tips I have learned to overcome this behavior:

1. If something bothers me and it isn't a super big deal or inconvenience, just take care of it. For example: if it's a couple of dishes that sit in the sink and bother me every time I see them, I just wash them. Then it stops bothering me. (However, if it is a regular issue for you and taking care of it doesn't fix your feelings, that needs to be addressed.)
2. Discuss the issue with a plan in mind. For example: "Hey, I noticed your guitar ends up staying in the living room after you play it and it is in my way. Would it be ok if I moved it into your room if I see it there?" (Practice your tone of voice.)
3. Sometimes it takes time to figure out why something bothers you, but when you do it can help a roommate be more sympathetic to you. Example: "I know this might be weird to you, but I grew up always turning the lights off in the hall before bed. Would it be ok with you if when you go to bed after me you turn that off?"
4. Be open to their point of view. Talk to them about what is going on. Sometimes, they might have something from

their childhood that affects why they do something. When you know that, you might become more understanding and less bothered by their behavior.

These behaviors are not exclusive to women. I have also seen these behaviors in men but in my experience, its usually a little different. Instead of talking to the roommate, they will just move out. And more than one married friend has been blindsided when her husband told her he was leaving, and she didn't even know there was an issue. Having regular conversations about how things are going helps. If these conversations aren't planned, they are not likely to happen. You can practice with roommates, setting aside time maybe once a month to check in with everyone, make sure things are going well and that everyone is getting the support they need.

Passive-aggressive and bottling are behaviors that are common amongst members of the Church. Each one of us is unique, with different experiences growing up that impact how we communicate with others. These are by no means the only behaviors that can be challenging to overcome in ourselves or in relationships with others. As we work on healthy relationships and communication skills now, we will be able to carry those skills and abilities into future relationships like with spouse and children.

Overcome The Culture Blues

How can we move the dial in a more positive direction when it comes to church culture and the single life? The most important thing we can do is to recognize and accept that there really isn't anything wrong with us. We are wonderful daughters of God with divine worth because we are His- no strings attached. Letting this belief fuel us with confidence will help us set righteous examples that will allow us to make a change for good. As we work on that, here are some more ideas on how to overcome culture clashes.

Be The Friend You Wish You Had

A complaint I hear sometimes from church members is that no one says "hi" to them at church and this makes them feel unwelcome and uncared for. I can sympathize. My sophomore year of college felt this way. Going to church was super hard because I didn't have any friends in my ward.

What I have learned is that it is hard for others to get to know me if I sneak in, don't speak to anyone, sneak back out, and never participate in activities. There are usually hundreds of people in Utah singles wards. And singles wards are constantly changing! If someone has been in a ward more than a year, it's unusual. No one knows who is new and who is not, and chances are the people you are expecting to say "hi" to you are just as new as you! So why not make it *your* responsibility to help ward members feel welcomed and loved?

That's the attitude I took after my mission. When I went to my first singles ward after coming home, I acted like I had been in the ward my whole life and started saying "hi" to everyone. As a result, I had a great Sunday and met a lot of people. Over my year there I made lots of friends, got a calling I loved, and greatly enjoyed my time there. I took the responsibility on myself to feel loved and find friends, and things worked out beautifully.

Look for Examples

I am so grateful for the examples of amazing Latter-Day Saint single women. This helps me feel validated and optimistic about my life and makes me strive to do and be better. I see people like Mallory Everton from BYU's Studio C, and Lindsey Stirling, single women in the Church who are slightly older than me, and who are famous because they are awesome and talented. I do not see them as a waste of space or as not good enough to be married, or anything negative. I see them as women who God can use to further His work, who are setting great examples and are a powerful force for good in the world! It's inspiring and it helps me remember that I too can use this time to do much good.

There are many great examples in the Church leadership too- Sheri Dew, Wendy Nelson, Kristen Oaks, some of my favorite women who have had great influence in the Church and either are not married or got married later in life. I personally gain a lot of strength from their examples.

There are many non-famous women who have also done this for me as well. I really look up to women who seem to be enjoying this unexpected life, and are strong in faith. One of these examples was a very talented and beautiful woman who came into my office with her husband. She was 31 years old and they were newly married, just a couple years older than I was at the time.

I met this woman when I was going through a particularly angst-y time of wishing I was married. But when she came in, vibrant, bold, with this whole dream career and as a volunteer for an organization she believed in, and she had found her husband at an age beyond the 'norm'. I was very impressed! She is an example of someone who didn't put their life on hold. She has been doing good and making beauty in the world, and it's just continuing as she enters this new chapter of being married. It did a lot to boost my spirits and help me get over my self-pity and move forward.

A Healthy Dose of Missionary Work

If you are feeling overwhelmed by church culture or forget what a blessing it is to be a member of the Church, try a dose of missionary work. That always helps me to see what is doctrine and what is culture, and better appreciate what I have even while surrounded by imperfect people and leaders.

When I was a freshman at SUU, I lived in a hall with about 30 girls. They were from all over, with super different backgrounds. I loved this! I loved pulling pranks on each other, and decorating our hall for the different holidays, and trying to work off our freshman 15 together. It was a blast.

Relationships

Something that was especially wonderful that year was getting to know my friend whom I will call Stephanie. We became super close, really quickly. She grew up in Utah, but didn't have much experience with The Church of Jesus Christ of Latter-Day Saints. One day she and I were out in the lobby when another girl was talking about a religion class. In the class they would spend 15 days learning about a religion, and then move on to another one. For some reason, mostly because it was funny, Stephanie and I decided to do 15 days of 'Mormonism', where I would teach her something about our Church each day for 15 days. It was all just fun and silly, until I was alone in my room that night. Then I thought about actually doing this, and what I could teach. At first I was overwhelmed and nervous, but then I remembered there are 13 articles of faith. I was excited to realize I was covered for most of the days!

The next morning, she came skipping up to my room and knocked on the door, wearing a South American-style winter hat with flaps that cover your ears, short shorts, and knee-high rainbow striped socks (a pretty typical outfit for her). When I opened the door, she came in and asked, "Alright! What's the first thing I need to know about Mormons?!" I took a deep breath, and then said, "We believe in God, the Eternal Father, and in His Son, Jesus Christ, and in the Holy Ghost." She blinked at me for a second, and then said, "No way?! So do us Catholics!" and then she went screaming down the hall, "Mormons believe in God, Jesus, and the Holy Ghost!" over and over again- not exactly the reaction I was expecting.

After a year of attending church and institute and facing some major trials, Stephanie was baptized. It was one of the best days of my life!

This experience taught me so much about what we take for granted as church members, how different our culture is, and that we really are a peculiar people. It took a year of institute for Stephanie to realize the gold plates were not something you eat on. I had never even thought about explaining that they were a book- it was something so obvious to me growing up as a member of the Church. I learned so much about what is essential as we met with the missionaries and learned the truths of the gospel. Another thing it taught me was that just because someone is baptized, doesn't mean they are suddenly at my level of understanding of doctrine and culture. It takes years of experiences to become more solid. I noticed that there were times before this experience when I judged others for what they wore to church etc., but after this experience I realized: maybe that girl wore *that* dress to church because that's the only dress she had, but she still wanted to come to church. Maybe she's new to church and doesn't know she is doing anything 'wrong' or that people might be silently judging her. I'm much more understanding, caring, and kinder to my fellow ward members after this experience.

Advocate for Other Singles

Sometimes it might be appropriate to stand up for each other. I had an experience with this one day at church when I was 27. It was a Fast and Testimony meeting, and a guy I had never seen before got up. He said something along these lines:

"Hi everyone, I am not in your ward. I am visiting my sister who is 27. I know none of you want to date her because she is so old. I don't blame any of you guys. She's past her time."

He continued on like that for a while and then walked out of the chapel. I was really upset and kept waiting for the bishop to get up and defend this poor sister in our ward. But it didn't happen, so finally, as the meeting was ending, I got up. I said something along the lines of:

"Hi everyone, my name is Elisa and I am a happy, thriving 27 year old. I love my life. I love the gospel. I know that age and marriage aren't tied together, and that everyone's path is unique, and all God's promises are available to each and every person here today". I didn't specifically address what the guy said, or condemn him. I just shared my testimony that God loves us and wants to bless us, regardless of our situation in life.

I don't remember what else I said, but as I backed away from the pulpit, the bishop whispered "thank you". I realized he probably wanted to say something but wasn't sure what to say, and I was able to help.

A Global Church

We do have a culture within our church. Our church is also one of the most global and encompassing groups that exists in the world. As cultures and families and countries all mix together there is conflict but there is also beauty. Sometimes if I don't feel like Conference or General Authorities of the Church are exactly addressing me, I try to remember that we are a global church, and that the General Authorities have the world's issues to address, not just mine. What I can do is keep working on being the best me, and make my personal culture one of love and care and service to others, and share that in my communities and neighborhoods no matter where I am, and in whatever phase of life I happen to be in.

Reagan O.'s Story

Some people seem to shudder at the thought of being older and single, especially in a church where getting married is a top priority and is a family-oriented gospel. When you get past the age of 25, people start asking questions and wondering why you're not trying "hard enough" to find a spouse. Here is my story, a girl who has tried and has yet to find "success". I am a 30-year-old Latter-Day Saint woman who always dreamed of being married and having children from a young age. I wouldn't say I was ever obsessed over the idea but always knew that that was my goal.

Church Culture

I had never had an "official" boyfriend until I was at the tender age of 18 as a freshman at BYU. My plan was to get an education and eventually marry the man of my dreams. When I was 18, young and still unsure of the world, I had no idea that I would be waiting 11 plus years to find the man I hope to marry and share eternity with. I always believed that I would find my spouse at BYU, we would graduate together, move away somewhere, and start a family. It never ever crossed my mind that that plan was not for me. At least, yet.

Throughout the last decade and more, since starting to date seriously for a husband, I have had my hardships, heartbreaks, and happy relationships along the way. The hardships of dating didn't fully hit until I was around 26. I was not married yet; I was still looking for someone and was soon to graduate from BYU in a year or two. That year, I did find someone or so, I thought. I fell in love with a man and we both wished to be married. We started making plans and we were practically engaged but without the official title and ring. We were contacting people and talking to our families about our future plans. About a month or so later, after beginning planning, our relationship started falling apart in which we decided to break up and not get married. This experience completely broke me. I felt like my plans had been ruined and I couldn't imagine anyone else that could make me happy ever again- or at least ever fall in love like that again. I went home for some time to heal from this broken relationship.

As my parents welcomed me with love, open arms, and deep sadness for my grief, I found a safe space in my home. Alas, going to church was another story. You see, no one knew that I was coming back from a really hard breakup and was trying to heal. When I went to church, I was hoping to find solace in the gospel, find protection with people that I grew up with and who love me, and to, of course, go to church like I always do.

Fortunately, and unfortunately, my experience at church taught me a lot about what not to say to someone when they are single. First off, I do not condemn anyone in the following experiences. I have forgiven them and have moved on. While at church, I had several offhand comments from others that I thought wouldn't say some of the things they did. For instance, one older woman asked me how dating was going and if I had found someone yet. I replied with a no and that I was still working on the dating sphere of my life. She asked how old I was and she proceeded to say "Well, you better hurry up because your eggs are drying up!" Then promptly walked away, leaving me completely devastated and helplessly standing in the foyer.

Then another woman, literally right after the first woman left, came up to me and asked how dating was going, then she said "Well, you better hurry up!". I was crestfallen. I couldn't have imagined anything worse than being told, after a broken off "engagement", that I needed to hurry up when it came to dating and marriage. I ran away crying in the bathroom and stayed there the rest of the time trying to pull myself together. These women had no idea what was going on in my life and wouldn't have known how hurtful their comments were. I told my parents afterward and they were just as shocked as I was.

Several years later, here I am, not married, and I can't get those comments out of my head. I can't say I have fallen in love again like that, but I have had and continue to have many moments of heartaches, disappointment, and dashed hopes. Those were only the first of many comments I have received throughout the years about needing to hurry or that I am getting old and should find a husband, or that I am not trying all that I can to find someone. Or of people giving me unsolicited dating advice. Or having people tell me that woman decrease in value as they grow older because it gets harder to produce children. These comments have been quite detrimental to my feelings of worth especially in moments of weakness. Satan attacks me with these comments after every rejection or "failed" relationship. It has been hurtful to remember those comments when I have yet to find "true happiness".

Church Culture

You are probably thinking so, what have you done with your life since that sad Sunday? I am here to tell you that I have lived. I keep moving forward. Those comments don't harm as much as they used to. I have worked to become my best self. Those that truly know me, know that I have been doing all that I can to find a spouse. I am not sitting and waiting around for a man to make my life happen or someone to sweep me off my feet. Not that I don't wish that would become true. I am making my life happen without an eternal companion. I have been abroad, I have served a mission, I have graduated BYU, and I have a full-time job, I am dating, learning new skills and hobbies, and spending time with friends and family that love me. I am doing it all.

Now, I can't say life and dating have been easy since that sad, sad Sunday a few years ago. I have had my disappointments and heartaches, my setbacks, my frustrations, my anger, and hatred of dating. I have had my feasts and famines. I have also had the joys of feeling cared for and being loved. How do I keep going? How do I keep trying? Despite the adversity and frustrations of continuing to grow older and not finding someone to grow old with. In a world where it seems unfair that someone who had already been married once, has yet found another love and is married again, while I can't even get married once. In a world where people that I used to babysit are getting married and having children of their own. In a world where most women my age are already on their 3rd or 4th child while I have none. In a world where I want to have children like my siblings and yet can't find a husband to help me with that. In a world where I ache to be in the same stage as my siblings. In a world where it seems like everyone else is moving on with their life and I seem to stay stagnant and in the same stage that I was in a decade ago as a new single adult.

Is there any hope? Can I have faith to continue to move forward? Do I trust God enough to lead me along the correct path? My answer is, YES! Absolutely there is hope and faith. God is guiding you! I have faith in God that He has a plan for me that is

Relationships

far better than what I have in mind. I can't imagine that God wouldn't want the best for me. I completely believe He does. It is different than what I had planned for me, and that is okay. It's not the end of the world. I would love to have a man, a companion, a husband in my life, of course, but I also don't need to be married to feel completely happy. I need a man to add to my happiness, not to be my only happiness. My Patriarchal Blessing tells me that I will have a spouse in this life and children in this life, so I hold onto that hope. I hold onto the hope that God will fulfill that blessing in my life. And if not, I will continue to have faith in God. I love that He has a better plan for me than what I could come up with on my own.

Many singles in the church, if not married by a certain age, tend to leave the church and the gospel they know. It is hard to be a part of a gospel that is so family oriented; I can see why single adults feel like they have no place in it. My advice, to those who are debating about leaving because they feel like they have better luck elsewhere, is to please stay. Everyone is needed in the church. Everyone is important in leading members to Christ. I could not imagine a better network than The Church of Jesus Christ of Latter-Day Saints. When moving around the country or world, you can almost always find other saints like you. What better way is there to meet and socialize with people who share your same ideals? You're not going to find those people in a bar. I keep thinking to myself that if I have lasted this long, with faith and hope, I can last a lot longer without a spouse. The church needs us and we need the church too. I have faith that God will lead me to where I need to be.

Of course, after a while, the millionth first date, the swiping up/down or left/right, the frustrations, and the failures get tiresome. Some days I continue to try and other days I give up. It is okay not to be okay and to take a break from dating. You're not going to be ruining your chances of meeting people if you take breaks. No matter what you do, God will be beside you and guiding you.

There have been moments where I have been angry with God and have been frustrated by the plan that is set for me. I cannot say that I have been perfectly happy with the way my life has turned out so far. Then, as always when I get frustrated and hurt, God always reminds me how much He loves and cares for me. I had an experience recently, where I was on a walk by myself and was feeling very defeated dating-wise. I prayed for peace and relief. As I was stewing in my misery, I had this overwhelming feeling of love and then the words in my mind said "I love you. Trust me". These words have filled me with hope. I will continue to trust in God and in His plan for me. Like I have said before, He knows what He is doing. Allow Him to lead you along where you are able to become the jewel He is polishing you to be. He gives me hope that there is someone whom He has in mind for me, and is polishing him for a little longer like He is doing to me.

    Something that my parents and I talk about all the time is that, yes, dating is hard and frustrating but look at how many life experiences and skills I am bringing to the table because of my continuous efforts to improve. I have a stable career, I have new talents and hobbies, and I am making connections with people. I am continuing to build my spiritual life, I am more emotionally capable of dealing with issues, and I feel like I am more prepared, because of those experiences, to be a wife and mother. If that is what I am looking for in a man, someone who is unceasingly growing and improving themselves, then I am going to be that too. I will be a much better wife than I could ever be, if I had married when I was younger. This knowledge still doesn't make it any easier, but I do hope that I am becoming a better wife and mother, and that I am exactly where God wants me to be.

    I have come to the realization that dating is hard, but life is also hard. I am not perfect in my faith in God. I am not even sure if my dream of marriage will ever come true, but I know that God loves me. I find comfort in that. Although my faith is not perfect, I trust God enough to believe that He knows what is best for me. He will lead me to what will make me the happiest, and to a point where I will be able to become my best self. Trust God. He knows what He is doing. Keep the faith, keep moving forward. God loves you and cares for you. I am not sure how much longer I will be single, but I do plan on living my best life, growing in all aspects to become more well-rounded, becoming more Christlike, and trusting in a God who loves me dearly. And as my wise mother shared with me; "If it is meant to work out, it won't fall apart".

Chapter 10
Dating

"Do you want capability, safety and security in...romance...? Be a true disciple of Jesus. Be a genuine, committed, word-and-deed Latter-day Saint. Believe that your faith has everything to do with romance, because it does." Elder Jeffrey R. Holland, "How do I love Thee?" *New Era,* Oct. 2003, 8.

Why is it so hard?

One of the main complaints I hear from single sisters in the church relates to dating culture. Sometimes single women move away from Provo because they think it will be better elsewhere, and perhaps there are some specific dating culture issues here. If I were to pin this down, I'd say it's feeling like we need to choose someone to marry for eternity, and we need to do it fast. And if you're in Provo, there are so many possible options that it's easy to *not* pursue a good relationship because you might meet another guy who is even better.

If you feel overwhelmed by these pressures, perhaps moving away from Provo or even Utah is the best solution for you. However, I think it's not necessarily a 'place' issue. I think the world overall has changed a lot regarding dating. The temptation is to look for something to blame when we aren't getting what we want (marriage), and "Provo Dating Culture" is often what gets blamed.

Dr. Scott Stanley from the University of Denver addressed BYU students and alumni February 7th, 2019 on BYU campus. He talked about what he calls "Dating in the Age of Ambiguity". He explained that while marriage happens more often in highly educated or highly religious communities, besides that, dating is the same. Here is what he said about dating today:

Where social norms and patterns used to exist to help signal and define the status of relationships as they progressed, there now exists a seemingly purposeful lack of defining signals in dating. Both fear and a lack of skill in communicating clearly have become driving factors in creating ambiguous, or not clearly defined relationships so people often fail to communicate what they want and don't want from their relationships. Secure commitments are clearly signaled...but ambiguity is the flavor of the age.

He goes on to say this ambiguity often results in one person being more committed than the other. From all my experience with dating and talking with roommates after dates, I couldn't agree more. This doesn't mean things are hopeless, it just means like all good things in life there is work to be done to become skilled at it.

Improve Your Dating Life

There are many things I have done to improve my dating life. I have found ways to take out the fear and stress in dating and make it fun. I look forward to going on dates and can be myself more. I am not desperately trying to please the guy, but rather getting to know him and letting him get to know me. Here are things that have helped me make dating relaxing and enjoyable.

Learn

I have spent time learning about men. I have read books, gone to seminars, and talked to them and asked them questions. I once took a class about how guys' brains work differently from ours. For example, when a guy asks you out, there is a high chance he thinks you are attractive. That never crossed my mind until I took this class. I have read *Men Are from Mars, Women Are from*

Dating

Venus more than once and it has helped me to understand behaviors in my family and why my guy friends or guys I like act the way they do. After talking to guys and learning about them, I'm also a lot less judgmental about guys playing video games so much. I used to get annoyed with what I considered excessive video gaming- probably because I have just one brother and he grew up with five sisters. But guys and girls have different needs. For me, understanding things is huge, and studying and researching has made guys less confusing. I also appreciate the things they do more. I don't just think "oh guys are all so dumb!" I see why things didn't make sense to me and what could make interactions more successful.

Flirting

When I first started dating and a guy gave me a compliment, I would either get really embarrassed if I liked him or defensive if I thought he was teasing. I have learned however, that many guys just joke around and it's fun, and that they say things that are cute even if they consider you just their friend. Being able to flirt back and have fun with it can be super rewarding. If you sense flirt mode is on, you go with it and say cute stuff back. It's just another skill to develop by practice. The single life is the best time to do this! If you say something dumb now, it's fine, because most guys you date you will never ever see again!

Be Happy

One way to attract men is to simply be happy. When I was 24, I learned that happiness is the most attractive trait you can have. I had heard about this, but until I experienced it for myself, I really didn't have a testimony of it. I started dating this guy, and it made me super happy: like giggly, easy-to-be-happy type of happiness. And guess what? In the two months we dated, I was asked out by four other guys. My record to that point had been about two dates per year. When I told this boyfriend about this, he said he calls it the "glow". You give it off when you are happy in a relationship, and it's attractive. I have found since that it is possible to have a glow even when you aren't in a relationship. Guys are attracted to that happiness. Who isn't? Just because you are married doesn't mean you are suddenly going to be happy all the time. Happiness is a skill to develop. Some of my favorite books on learning this skill are *The Happiness Advantage*, and *The Happiness Project*.

Be Yourself

I was dating a guy a number of years ago. It was kind of an office romance- we met through work though he was at a different building than me. One night he was working late, so I went over to his office to wait for him to finish. As we were walking out, I saw an open janitor closet. I thought to myself: if this man were my husband, I would pull him into that closet to kiss him. The idea appealed to my sense of humor. And then I had another thought right after: why couldn't I do that now? How would I know if this guy was right for me unless I acted like myself and saw how he responded? So… I did. And it made me laugh and he did too… nervously. It taught me a lesson: being myself makes me happy and lets the person I am dating really get to know me. Can you imagine if I married a guy who didn't appreciate all my quirkiness? You want to know those things in advance.

One of the most common phrases people say is, "I'm so awkward". Instead of using this as an excuse to not talk to a guy or get someone's number, try seeing that the silly things you do are part of who you are, and it will be very endearing to some guy someday. Lean in to your uniqueness, and see it as a strength.

First Dates

As I talked to a lot of women in preparation for this book, many asked me to address the issue of dating- especially first dates. Why are they so hard? How can you get rid of the pressure and make dating bearable?

Dating

After doing lots of pondering, I think there is pressure because dating can be the means to the greatest anticipated life and eternity change of all time. It would be weird if there *wasn't* pressure. So the issue is more around: how do we make it a relaxing and good experience that is edifying and helpful to us and the other person?

As a financial professional, I used to get so nervous before meeting with a client. All I could see was that I was trying to sell them something, making them buy something they didn't actually want or need. This attitude definitely repelled people from working with me. I would sweat and stutter and be unable to give good answers. But over time, and with lots of practice, I have learned that all I am doing is listening to what people want, and then helping them to get that if I have what they need. If not, we all move on.

I feel like this can apply to dating. You aren't trying to sell yourself. You don't want to be a fit for every guy. You are a woman with high value, and you are looking to connect with just one man, who sees the real you and you see the real him and you're happy together. There's nothing wrong with you if a date doesn't work out. Sometimes even if you feel it is right, the other party has emotional baggage or challenges they aren't yet capable of working on.

Some things that have helped me to be a less anxious dater:

1. Remember that not every date needs to lead to marriage. Just have fun. It can be an opportunity to practice being my authentic self.
2. Remember that God is bigger than me- if I really mess up the date but it is meant to be, God will fix it. He parted the red sea; He can make things work for me.
3. Dancing to some pump-up music before you go is very helpful to release nerves.
4. It's ok to not know if I am into the guy after one date. I am allowed to go on a couple of dates before I

decide if I am into him or not and want to keep getting to know him.
5. I am allowed to say no to things whenever I feel uncomfortable. This applies to before or during a date.
6. Remember that if a date goes terribly, I will have a hilarious story to tell afterwards.

I was brought up to always say yes when a guy asks you out, unless you have a gut feeling or good reason not to. This has led me to sometimes saying yes to guys that were definitely not a fit for me. When some guys hear you say yes, they assume you are crushing on them like they have been crushing on you. They might even start trying to talk to you regularly as soon as you say yes. In these situations when I really know it is not a fit, I will let them know that I am happy to go on a friend date if they would like, but it won't be more than that. When they know my intentions and feelings, things work out and I don't have to ghost anyone or move out of my ward.

One day, you will go on your last first date ever. And the crazy part is you won't know it is your last first date for quite some time! But you will look back and remember that day for the rest of your life no matter how good or bad, traumatic or boring it was. Because of this, I try to not hate first dates so much. For now, the adventure is to continue to go on first dates. But one day they will all turn into wonderful (and/or hilarious) memories.

<u>Communicate</u>

This age of ambiguity creates a dating world of fear and inability to communicate wants. To change that, start by deciding what you want in your relationships (what defines a date for you, what are your boundaries and expectations), and communicating that. I had one friend who actually had a paper listing her dating expectations that she would give to guys. She said she knew it was unorthodox, but after I went to her wedding I stopped thinking she was crazy. This practice isn't necessary for everyone, but she was obviously very clear on her expectations; she communicated that to the men she dated and it worked out favorably.

We forget sometimes that men are trying to figure out this dating world at the same time that we are. I have told guy friends that I hate it when guys text me forever on Mutual instead of asking me out. I've also told them I hope they actually ask out girls instead of just text them. And every guy friend responds with, "Well I used to ask a girl out right away, but then girls freak out and say I'm moving too fast!" They also tell me girls are less likely to say yes to dates if you ask without getting to know them first. Thus, guys expect to spend a lot of time initially, just 'hanging out' or texting with the girl, so they can get to know each other before dating, to avoid an angry girl situation. Obviously, not all girls are the same, and guys are dealing with that.

A lot of guys feel like they are walking on eggshells in this world of dating. Most are not cruelly trying to take advantage of you or play with your emotions. Like you, they have insecurities and fears and struggle to communicate what they want and don't want. They worry about how they should act- should they open the door for you? Some women will get mad if they do, other women will get mad if they don't. Some men have family or personal pressure to be able to provide financially for a family before seriously dating. Then there's just plain fear of being rejected.

A thing I hear a lot from women when they are disappointed in a how a man treats her is "he should know!". The woman doesn't tell him how she wants to be treated, but expects him to treat her a certain way. Here's something to keep in mind: you know how we always come home and talk about our dates? Well guys don't typically do that. So where are they learning dating etiquette? Feedback from the girls they date. If you don't say what you want, it is unlikely that you will get this. I know many women feel this is unromantic, but you might just be surprised how he steps up once he knows exactly what you want.

Relationships

There was a guy I dated once; after our third date, I invited him to kiss me, which he did. I then started to assume we were boyfriend and girlfriend. However, after I heard him tell someone he wasn't dating anyone, I realized that for him, kissing didn't mean we were official. The next time he tried to kiss me, I told him that I don't kiss guys unless we are officially in a relationship. He took some time, and then asked me to be his girlfriend. Now we were on the same page. I didn't have to wonder about the status of the relationship and knew that he was committed to me.

This brings up another thing- I think a lot of times girls are afraid that a guy won't like them if they communicate the standards they want. It's not true. And if it is true, he is not the one for you. When you communicate your standards, in my experience most guys are really respectful, even if they think differently than you. But if you never make your standards known, then unless they think exactly like you, you can expect that there will be differences in standards, preferences, and everything else. And here's the reality: no guy (or person) will ever think exactly like you.

Everyone is different when it comes to dating. You have personal preferences whether it's to have the guy walk you to your door or meet them at the location separately. Understand that your preferences are different than others, and unless communicated a guy will never know.

What Not To Do

There are a couple of things I see women do that *don't* work. I have experienced them both myself. If you are experiencing either of these situations, please don't just assume that things will work out differently for you. Recognizing unhealthy relationships and moving on is an important relationship skill.

Waiting Around

Sometimes because dating seems so terrible, I see girls waiting around for a certain guy just hoping he will finally ask her out. Here's what it looks like. There's this guy that you like, and you talk *a lot*, but he just doesn't ask you out. But you know that you two are meant to be, because obviously you are talking every day. Lots of time goes by, and even though you feel like you talk enough to be in a committed relationship, things haven't moved any further. He is just not taking the leap!

What usually comes of this situation: nothing. I have yet to see a relationship like this work out. What I have seen is that guys will act when they are ready to. Sure, all guys have levels of shyness and anxiety. But if years pass and he is not asking you out, you probably need to let go of the relationship. Focus on other things in your life. Who knows? Doing other things (especially with other guys) might make him realize he is interested in a relationship with you. Even if *he* never comes around, don't ever tell yourself he is your only chance. There are a lot of good guys out there. Something my dad says is "don't waste time with someone else's husband". Now that isn't a hard and fast rule- we can learn a lot from any relationships and experiences. It means don't rot away in a relationship that isn't moving. Take a break, do other things, meet other people.

Obsessing

Have you ever found yourself praying like this:

Dear God,
So I met this guy, and he's pretty cute. And obviously I don't really know him yet, but he seems to be a really great guy. So please help me not to say anything dumb around him. I think maybe he might possibly be interested in me. If he is, please *please* let him ask me out! Help me not be intimidating to him. Help me not freak out and to just be normal around him. And please, if things start to work out, help me to stay cool, and be myself, and just have fun with him. And if he is the one, God, please let it work out! But help me just to enjoy the moments with him, help me not to get anxiety, or overly clingy, or push him away, or shut him out.

Help me to make this natural. And if he is the one, please help me to know that. Please give me a sign or help me to know somehow for sure that he is the one. And if we do get married, please bless our marriage to be strong. Help us to work together through all obstacles, no matter what happens. Please bless it all to work out and help us to never get a divorce. Oh God, please help us to never get a divorce! Please help us to make it work! And then please help us to have an awesome life together where we can grow old together and be cute grandparents together and have a full, happy, and complete life....

    From meeting a guy to the end of a life together-it's ridiculous right? But how many times have I done something like this, or have I heard my friends say similar things? You are definitely not alone if you have ever felt something like this. It helps to find the humor.

    When you meet someone, there is nothing wrong with feeling optimistic about the relationship. It is okay to imagine being together or things working out but avoid letting it become an obsession. Driving past his house when it is out of your way or spending hours coming up with perfect, detailed texts to send him is not healthy. It's hard, because you just want something to work out so badly, you create it in your mind. But changing your work schedule on Fridays just in case he asks you out, if he has never asked you out before, is going too far. Do yourself a favor and fill your life with other meaningful activities and relationships instead.

Pornography

    Pornography is something that comes up often in dating. If talking about pornography is a trigger for you, skip this section. I do want to address this, though, as it is something that comes up a lot in dating.

Dating

The idea of dealing with pornography in a relationship can be terrifying because we know that it is evil and one of Satan's tools to destroy families. Let's start out by talking about what porn is not. It is not proof that a man doesn't respect women or is not satisfied with a relationship partner. It is not proof that someone is unworthy of love, undeserving of a relationship, or a bad person.

Most people who have pornography habits or addictions are good people. It often starts from curiosity – things like wanting to know where babies come from. If a child isn't taught this from their parents, it is so easy to look things up on the internet and YouTube these days and end up down a rabbit hole of destruction. The marketing world is against young people too. I went to a seminar for Fight the New Drug, an organization that is working to spread awareness about the harms of pornography use, and they said that many porn sites are currently targeting 11-year-old girls. All the people I have talked to that struggle with this started out super young, and in a very innocent way.

Once the world of porn is opened up to a person, it is hard to turn it around. That is how addictions work, and why we are taught to not even have one sip of alcohol or one cigarette. It's also I believe why the Church teaches the importance of having virtuous thoughts. Thoughts are what lead to actions and one internet search for porn can end up causing an addiction. Once the brain is triggered by something so powerful, it becomes a stress reliever. One of the world's leading addiction researchers, George Koob, said this about addiction:

> "...when a person is suffering from addiction, their stress response and their addiction become intertwined in unhealthy ways. Instead of driving them to respond appropriately to life's challenges, stress and anxiety will instead drive them to their addiction. Likewise, anytime they're cut off from their addiction, they will experience intense feelings of stress and anxiety (also knowns as withdrawal), creating an unhealthy cycle in

which all roads seem to lead to the same addictive substance or behavior." (Koob G.F. (2013) Addiction is a Reward Deficit and Stress Surfeit Disorder. Frontiers in Psychiatry, 4, 72.)

It's like getting drunk or taking drugs. It takes away the pain, sends pleasure to the brain. The problem is, it is extremely hard to turn off that pleasure signal once it has been turned on. If you have never had that space activated in your brain, it's very hard to explain. Here's my best attempt: imagine being extremely hungry. You know when you get really hungry and you can't think about much else? And now let's say it's manic- where you *really* can't think of anything else except feeding that hunger for food. Your body starts to itch for it and you start to be in pain and literally feel that if you don't eat something soon you are going to explode. That's what it's like. Pornography is the relief to this hunger that has been stirred.

Men you date, you yourself, or roommates may be turning to porn as a means to deal with loneliness, stress with school, or any other pain from life. Many users don't even realize they are doing it as a stress reliever. I am not an expert on this subject, but I do know there are lots of resources available to get help. Because I think this impacts dating, I am focusing on how to deal with it in that context.

When should you bring this subject up? Probably not on a first date, but also not after you are engaged. You can pray for guidance and help and ask trusted leaders. For many men it is much easier for them to discuss this when they feel trust and confidence in a relationship.

Make sure you have a good discussion about it, and probably more than one discussion. Don't assume you know exactly what they are talking about if they say they have seen porn. How often does it happen? What are their triggers for it (do they know their triggers)? What are they doing to work on this? A man

Dating

who tells you he has struggled but is working to put up defenses for himself against pornography is likely a righteous man.

Here's what you can do when someone tells you they struggle with pornography. First, tell them how proud you are of them for telling you. Do not be disgusted by them; show them extra love with a hug or something. Tell them you know they can beat this and that you will support them! If they are ready to go to a recovery program or talk to the bishop, offer to go with them. If they don't already have plans for those things, invite them to do so, but don't try and force them. Assure them you are a support and will be available for them.

In today's world, pornography is one of the biggest tools Satan has to make us feel alone, isolated, and unworthy. It affects men and women. It is very difficult to completely avoid it, no matter how hard you try. Even without seeking it, often ads or popups will appear that contain pornography. So let's be there for each other in this battle with Satan. If a brother or sister has been wounded, don't reject them. Rather, let's lift them up, guide them to the Master Healer, and do what we can to help.

Being open and talking about pornography is the first step towards healing, and it feels wonderful. Satan is the only one trying to convince us to keep our struggles a secret, telling us we are unworthy of help or love. The reality is that most people have been or currently are dealing with the effects of pornography in one way or another. God wants you to be free of your sins and hurt, no matter how bad it is. That's why He sent His Son Jesus Christ, so that you and those you love can be healed from these sins- even repeated sins. The Atonement of Jesus Christ can also heal you if you feel you have been hurt by pornography or abuse through a partner or loved one. I have a testimony of that and am grateful for the access to healing.

Relationships

In Love With The Man Or With Love?

Through all my dating experience, I have learned it is important to recognize the difference between being in love with a person and being in love with love. Sometimes you get an emotional high simply because you are in a relationship. It's *easier* to be happy and downright giddy at times when in a relationship. This can make it tricky when you are trying to figure out if you are in love with the person. It's important to give relationships enough time, and make sure that you are actually in love with the person and not just the fact that you are in a relationship. How to do this? There are a couple of things that can help you:

1. What do your family/friends say about them? Are there red flags they mention? Do they all dislike the person? Give this feedback from people you care about serious consideration.
2. List their good and bad qualities. Doing this with a person you trust (not the significant other) can help make sure you are being realistic. Once you have the list, "take the person out". Meaning, look at the list as if it were a dating profile for someone else. Would you date someone like that? What if you were to marry someone with those qualities? Would you be ok with that? ("They will change" is not an acceptable answer if you are uncomfortable with the profile here. Read the book *How to Avoid Falling in Love with a Jerk* for more info on this.)

There are people that meet and quickly get married. I'm sure you know someone that this has happened to, and they are still happily married 30 years later. I believe this is connected to the guidance of the spirit. God knows what a person will be like down the road where we can't. He can help confirm in our minds and hearts that something is right. Not everyone gets a big: *Yes, he's the one for you*, and actually this is good, because agency is such an important part of life. But I have had a couple of friends confess to me that they were warned by the spirit that they *shouldn't* marry someone, and they did anyway (usually scared to call everything off especially after so much money by family had been spent) and then ended up getting divorced. The more we can focus on what God thinks above anyone else, the better our decisions will be.

Now, this is not true of all divorced Latter-Day Saints. There could be reasons that made a marriage right at the time, and then things changed. We really can't judge. The point is, be careful of falling in love with love when you are in a relationship, as opposed to falling in love with a person, or following the promptings of the spirit.

You Can Do This

Once after a breakup, Satan tried to convince me that I blew my one chance to get married. He's a tricky one, but I know that if a thought makes me feel hopeless or worthless, it is not from God. I knew that God had spoken to me when I was worried about breaking up before it happened, and He eased my anxious soul. I chose to listen to God and that helped me feel better and move forward.

If you really wanted to just get married, you could. There are guys on dating apps you could propose to on a first date and go to Vegas with today. But you choose not to do that. You choose to wait for a temple-worthy, righteous, and loving man who adores you. Remember this when you feel desperate. You aren't just trying to get married. You are working on creating an eternal relationship because you are a valuable daughter of God, and you are worth having the best.

Dating is hard, but so is marriage. As we work on the skills and tools of good and healthy dating, we will be that much more prepared for marriage. You can do this! You can date like a queen and feel good about your interactions. It is possible to feel confident and enjoy dates. I am rooting for you!

Relationships

Challis T.'s Story

A few years ago I had this boyfriend who I was in love with. I fell fast and hard and that had never happened to me before. He made me so happy! After about a month of dating he was offered a job. It had excellent benefits and *really* good pay, but it was temporary, only about 6 months, and it was on the other side of the world, literally! When he told me about it I just cried. I tried not to but I didn't want him to go.

After he left we tried staying in contact. I was unable to call him but he could call me on a special call line. Slowly the phone calls became less frequent and after about two months I stopped hearing from him at all. To be honest the phone calls did not fill me with joy the way being in his presence did and the relationship died. I was heartbroken.

I remember one night pouring my sorrow out to Heavenly Father in prayer. Not just my sorrow about our distant relationship, but the feelings that I was not worth it, that somehow I was at fault for him wanting to go so far away from me. I let Heavenly Father know that I was feeling like there was something wrong with me and that I was somehow not worthy to be married and that is why I was not finding someone willing to take that step with me.

This prayer went on for hours as I talked about everything I was feeling and questioning. After talking about my struggles I started to talk about what my future had in store. Finally I let him know that if being single for the rest of my life is what he had planned for me then I would learn to live with that and still do everything I could to remain close to him. I promised that I would remain by his side throughout my life no matter what. With that promise I felt peace. Not a spiritual confirmation that this is what my life would be, but a bone deep appreciation from my Heavenly Father letting me know he was pleased with my willingness to leave this matter in his hands, and a promise that he would always be there for me and take care of me.

Dating

I know that my Heavenly Father loves me more than I can possibly understand. He wants me to be happy and will do everything in his power to give me that happiness and joy, if I will just remain by his side. I have complete faith that one day I will have an amazing husband and many wonderful children who I will teach to love the Lord and use the Atonement to find joy and happiness in this life.

In the Oct 2012 session of General Conference Elder Uchtdorf provided this council: "So often we get caught up in the illusion that there is something just beyond our reach that would bring us happiness: a better family situation, a better financial situation, or the end of a challenging trial. The older we get, the more we look back and realize that external circumstances don't really matter or determine our happiness. We do matter. We determine our happiness."

I was reminded that even if I was married to an amazing priesthood holder, and we had the picture-perfect family I so desperately want, that would not mean I would be happy. Even a worthy priesthood holder can hurt your feelings and those picture-perfect children would not always be picture-perfect. After all a picture-perfect moment generally only lasts for about five minutes before a child is pinching a sibling or your wonderful husband is saying he is too busy to help.

We determine our happiness. Knowing these moments will come does not stop us from wanting those 5 minutes of picture-perfect family home evenings, prayers, and loving husband and children to hug.

What we have to do, no matter where we are in life, with or without the desired family, is take our hearts and happiness to the Lord. He will protect our happiness better than any imperfect husband, family, or bank account ever could.

Give your happiness to the one who has proven his immense love for us by giving his life on Calvary and providing us with the Atonement to guide us through every hard time no matter how hard, how long, or how complicated it may seem to us it is not to him.

Regardless of the changes in our circumstances or the lack of the desired change, if we give our hearts and the protection of our joy to Jesus Christ, we will not have anything in this life to regret. In His great love for us He has prepared a way for all of the righteous to have the opportunity to make covenants. I know this can be hard to hear. Many times when I hear this I think: "But I don't want to wait for my husband to come after this life. I want it now. Here on earth where I can raise children and feel complete."

When we come to this wall remember the perfect example of our Savior in Matthew 26:42 "...O my Father, if this cup may not pass away from me, except I drink it, thy will be done."

Do what you can now. Make choices that will take you closer to Christ regardless of what others say or are doing. Follow your Savior and live the best life you can serving in the gospel wherever you are and giving as much of yourself as you can. Help others. Remind them where to find true and lasting happiness. Each time you share your testimony of the Savior and his plan of happiness you will feel that joy a little more in your life.

Remember that you are an eternal creature living in an imperfect world. God knows and loves you. If what you want is to have a future family, remember to pray for them. Pray for your future husband that he will have the peace of the gospel and the guidance of the Holy Ghost so that you can be led to each other. Pray that you are learning the things you need to know to be the best wife and mother you can be.

Remember that families are eternal with a temple sealing and that you can be a blessing to your future family now by seeking knowledge, spiritual guidance, and current experience.

Section 4
Personal Peace

Where can I turn for peace?
Where is my solace
When other sources cease to make me whole?
When with a wounded heart, anger, or malice,
I draw myself apart,
Searching my soul?

He answers privately,
Reaches my reaching
In my Gethsemane, Savior and Friend.
Gentle the peace he finds for my beseeching.
Constant he is and kind,
Love without end.

-Where Can I Turn for Peace? *LDS Hymn Book*, 1973 IRI

Chapter 11
Overcoming Fears

"Correct knowledge of and faith in the Lord empower us to hush our fears because Jesus Christ is the only source of enduring peace." – Elder David A Bednar, "Therefore They Hushed Their Fears", *Ensign*, May 2015

Worry and Anxiety

From the time I was eight years old, I knew I would serve a mission. I loved the idea of traveling to a new country, and I also loved God. I watched movies about being a missionary. After I got my call, I spent hours learning about Bolivia and looking at pictures online. I knew people lived in little huts and wore traditional clothes. I looked forward to braving the jungles and converting the hearts of all the people I would meet.

I was not prepared to live that way, though. For some reason, I had this *expectation* that I would live somewhere that was like North America- with plumbing, air conditioning, and no bugs. I thought the only time I would experience Bolivia would be when I would leave my apartment. I didn't tell myself this or consciously think it. It was just that having only ever lived in or been in the USA, I didn't really have context for anything else. It wasn't until my Bolivian companion picked me up, and we got into a taxi driven by a Bolivian, that I started to panic.

Where in the world was I? What was I thinking coming here? The moment I walked out of the church after getting my mission companion assignment, all ability to communicate disappeared. Despite my best efforts for the nine weeks in the MTC, I did not speak Spanish, and she did not speak a word of English. I was terrified to not be able to communicate.

Overcoming Fears

Then we arrived at our 'house', which was actually a room connected to the back of someone's house. You had to go outside to get to the bathroom and 'kitchen', and there were spiders and cockroaches and lizards and sometimes mice in all three of those locations. It was so hot. I could feel my hair growing in the humidity.

Then there was the rain. The rain in Bolivia is incredible. If we were outside and we saw black clouds on the horizon, we had to *run* home. Even then, we'd usually be shin deep in water by the time we got home. In my first area, after a rainstorm there were almost always a couple of dead mice around our patio. In other areas there would be frogs everywhere or giant Hercules beetles that would fall dead out of trees after the rain. The jungle is a crazy place!

I was scared of everything. I was afraid of a cockroach or mouse touching me in my sleep and I was terrified that a poisonous spider would bite me. I was scared to tract new streets- anyone could jump out and murder me! Wild dogs were everywhere, and we would be chased about once a week. People had diseases and sicknesses I hadn't even heard of. I was scared of letting down God or the people or my family. What if my companion decided to leave me one day? I didn't have a phone or money or know how to get back to our house. What if we got in a taxi and they drove us wherever they wanted to take us? I was scared of being raped or kidnapped and killed. I couldn't shake these thoughts. All day long the terrors and possibilities were repeated through my mind, never leaving me a second of peace.

Anxiety is something I had dealt with before my mission. I had some natural anxiety medicine that I had brought with me. However, for some reason, it didn't cross my mind during those first months of my mission that what I was feeling was anxiety, so I didn't take any of my meds. This time the anxiety had gone beyond anything I had ever experienced before. I was terrified and in shock, and it didn't let up from morning until night. Some days I would explode into uncontrollable sobbing fits for *hours* and my poor companion just looked miserable, not knowing what to do.

Two things kept me going during this time. One was Fernando- the young man we were teaching. The second was these recurring dreams of running away from my mission and swimming back to Utah and feeling disappointed for the rest of my life because I didn't finish my mission.

I have been a worrier my whole life. I didn't realize that when I was little, but I definitely was. When I couldn't see my mom for a couple of seconds at the store, I would run up to the front to have them call her on the intercom (I'm sure she loved that). When we went to Disneyland when I was 11, I had a hard time enjoying it because I repeatedly counted my family members in my mind so as not to lose any of them. People didn't talk about anxiety back then. Growing up, I called it worrying.

I remember one time I was reading the scriptures as a 12-year-old. I didn't want to be such a worrier and I was hoping to figure out how to not worry so much. I don't think I actually prayed for help, but I remember at some point reading about the stripling warriors. As I read, the spirit taught me that I could be a Worrier or a Warrior. That helped me a lot in changing how I thought. At that point, I really made a shift to think and be like a warrior, not a worrier. Just that thought change helped me to better control my worrying for several years.

However, as I grew older, I had various life experiences that put me back into worrying mode. My life has often been like that. I struggle with anxiety, and then with the help of God and hard work, I am able to overcome it. I wish there was a magic way to always stay out of that difficult place, but life is hills and valleys, not a straight road. I find things that help me along the way. Kirk Duncan has a CD where he talks about imagining opening up your head, taking out your brain, and cleaning it off every day. Things like this help me out when I find myself going to that place of fear again. If there is something big and looming in my distant future, but there isn't much I can do about it in the moment, I have learned to set up a future date when I am allowed to worry about that thing. That way it's not allowed to continually cause me anxiety and fear.

Fear, worry, anxiety… have been part of my life as far back as I can remember. There are different levels of each. I hope to specifically address fears that are generally the same for all single women. The *levels* of stress and anxiety for each person or even day-to-day might vary drastically, however. If you ever feel like your fear/stress is at an unmanageable level- meaning it is keeping you from doing basic tasks like working, eating, sleeping, etc., I recommend getting professional help.

Fear You Missed Your Chance

The idea that you had one chance to get married and blew it is terrifying, but a real fear many single women have at some point. One thing that helps me is to remember that through Jesus Christ there is nothing I can do to mess things up so badly that He can't fix it. Even if you do blow it with a guy that could have been a potential husband, things aren't over for you. God is a God of second chances, and we will always get to try and try again.

One time I felt like I had ruined my chances with a guy. As I was feeling sad about it, I talked to my sister. She asked me an important question: was I doing everything God asked me to do? At first I thought, "yes of course!" but then the spirit brought to my mind the fact that God had repeatedly told me to "Stop and stand still" and wait upon Him. I realized that I had not been doing this well, despite being repeatedly told this for over a year. I was pretending I was being patient, yet I was trying to force this guy into a relationship with me.

I was frustrated and sad because I had not been heeding the promptings I had been given. However, something wonderful happened as I let go. I started thinking of all the amazing things I could do while being single. That's when I got the idea to write this book. It's when I really started considering being a foster mom, and what led me to make a goal of buying a house. I became so full of passion for many different things I could do while single. I have my whole life and eternity to focus on my husband and kids.

One of the reasons I struggled so much with letting go and waiting on the Lord, is that I feared missing my husband. I was afraid that somehow he would pass me by and I would miss him. But the Lord won't let that happen if you trust Him. Once I talked to a man who is a Sealer at the temple. He said he was doing Sealings for the dead one night when a girl and a guy walked in. He thought they were together, so he started writing them both down under the guy's last name. They quickly responded that they were not together and didn't even know each other. He apologized and they continued. During the session, he accidentally called them up as a couple. She kindly corrected him again, the sealer apologized, and they went on. Then it happened again. This time she started to correct him, gave up halfway through, but this time when they sat down they were smiling at each other. A fourth time, this sealer called them up as a couple accidentally. This time when they sat down, they were holding hands. They left together.

Hearing this experience reminded me that God can literally do anything and He will work whatever miracles are necessary for your life. Your job is to do your best to become closer to God so you will have the inspiration to follow His plan for you. It's to learn and do the things you need to do to return to Him and to help others accomplish that as well. If I get busy doing a whole bunch of good in the world that I don't see my husband around, God can make a miracle happen like he did for that couple at the Temple. I don't have control over making a man fall in love with me. I do have control over growing my relationship with God.

Fear of Missing Out

Do you have FOMO? It's an acronym for: Fear of Missing Out. What if you get married only because you are afraid of falling behind or missing out? It might not be obvious that you are dating someone for that reason at first. The way to tell is if you find yourself wanting to stay with someone because your friends are dating and getting engaged and you want it too. If that is your motivation, as opposed to really enjoying getting to know the person you are with and seeing a long-term relationship, you're probably not setting yourself up for success. A lasting marriage needs to be made on a foundation of faith in Jesus Christ, not fear of being alone or fear of not keeping up with your friends.

What about fear of not being able to go to every social event just in case *he* is there? That can become stressful quickly. I have a sister who is a great example of *not* having FOMO. She became the national student chef of the year after just one year of culinary school. Part of her secret for success was her ability to say no to hanging out when she needed to work, and going to sleep early even when other people were going out.

I was definitely not this way when I was in college. I was always the last one to go to my dorm room to sleep and I paid for it in the long run. I didn't become as successful in my major as I could have until I came back from my mission and actually spent time practicing my music instead of just playing around all day and night. There will always be time for fun even if you set aside time for the important things you want. If you do important things first, you won't miss out on anything.

I also had a friend once who worried constantly that she wouldn't be available for her family if they needed her. She didn't even go to college for fear of not being able to be there for her family. It *is* important to be there for your family. But don't hold yourself back from progression because of fear. Your family and friends would probably be sad if they realized they were the reason you didn't become your best self. Find a balance. It may take some time, but it pays off in the long run.

Sometimes all this missing out can seem excruciatingly unfair, especially as more and more time passes. Holidays and family get-togethers start becoming painful. Mother's Day can be very hard despite your best efforts to stay optimistic. Somehow something always manages to get you down. Luckily, Jesus Christ knows how we feel and he sends prophets and apostles to help us with the challenges we face. In his talk, "Infuriating Unfairness", Elder Dale G. Renlund of the Quorum of the Twelve Apostles says, "In the eternities, Heavenly Father and Jesus Christ will resolve all unfairness." Life isn't fair, but how grateful I am to know and trust that God knows it's unfair, and one day He is going to repair every injustice.

Until that day comes, though, we need to practice faith and patience. Something that helps me with this is really focusing on the present moment. Nothing beats future-thinking anxiety like learning how to enjoy today. For many of us this isn't natural; it's a skill or ability we've got to develop. We are much better at worrying about every possible thing that could go wrong. All the time God says to me, "Peace, be still". Worrying or panicking is never something God tells me to do. The more I learn to let go of the fear of the future and live in the moment, the better my life is.

There are things you can do to help you live in the moment. One thing I learned in therapy is to take a moment to connect with your senses. Look at the things you can see around you. Listen to what you can hear right now. What can you smell? Touch things around you. If you have a mint or something else edible nearby, put it in your mouth and taste it. These things bring you back to the present moment which can be very helpful if you are really stressed. Sometimes I even forget to breathe. Focusing on breathing is the most in-the-moment thing you can do, and sometimes all you need is one deep breath to get yourself back on track.

Fear of Never Getting Married

The thing that has really helped me in my battle against anxiety is remembering *in the moment* of stress, fear, or sadness, that the emotion I am currently experiencing is temporary and will not last forever. When I am able to remember this, I can relax at least a little bit and put things into perspective.

Your mind is powerful. Have you ever heard of the law of attraction? It means that you attract to your life what you are seeking. If you think you are ugly, you will look for evidence to prove this to yourself. If you keep saying you are going to be a cat lady one day, your subconscious picks up on that. It will start helping you achieve what you are saying.

I used to think if I planned on getting married, then I could be setting myself up for disappointment and sadness when/if it didn't happen. It felt safer to just plan to *not* get married. Then if I did end up getting married, that would be a super nice bonus to life! I wanted to avoid regret and unnecessary pain. But living like that did not feel good. I wasn't happy. So, what was I avoiding? Nothing.

With the help of a couple of Priesthood blessings, I started to try to see marriage as something that *will* come to me. One blessing said I needed to imagine being with God, with my husband and kids. This was interesting advice, and I realized that I could not picture that. I decided to draw a picture of my future husband and I with our kids. It was kind of weird at first, but then I started thinking about it- not just me returning to God at the end of my life, but being with my husband. I started thinking about names for my kids. This picture is in one of my drawers, because it's so personal. It motivates me to be a better person.

I also started my own wedding fund. When I can, I put a little bit of money in a savings account specifically for my wedding. This has helped me think of my wedding as something that I am preparing for that will happen. It's another little way to change my thinking to make marriage seem more real. In addition, priesthood blessings have told me I should prepare now to be a mom. At first I put that on hold because I thought, "what are the chances that will ever happen?" Now I try to do things with that counsel in mind. I try to live my life with the belief in mind that I will be getting married, even while progressing alone today.

Sometimes fear leaves me frustrated that things aren't in my control. I don't want to let go and trust God, because I want things to happen my way and I *fear* if I let go and trust God, that I won't get what I want- mostly a husband. Because I don't feel like God is giving me directions on who my husband is or where he is, I try to *make* it happen. And when I can't make things happen the way I think they should, I get frustrated.

But good has come through these struggles. I have come closer to my Savior, and I have learned that *every time* I let go of fears and frustrations and trust in him and in my Heavenly Father, I grow closer to them and to the person I want to be. It motivates me to keep trying and never give up. I trust that God is helping me and that He wants my happiness more than anything else.

How to Overcome Fears

I have made some suggestions for overcoming anxieties and fears. Here are a few more ideas of things that have proven helpful for me.

Jars

Make a memory jar. The idea is to fill it with good memories throughout the year. Then, at the end of the year, you can look back at all your wonderful experiences and accomplishments. The first year I tried this, I did it instead of making New Year's resolutions, because I was really depressed around that time, and I just couldn't bring myself to make goals. All year as good things happened to me, I'd write them on a piece of paper and put it in the jar. New Year's the next year was fabulous, because I read everything and felt so good about myself! The next year I did it again, but I also made resolutions. All those great memories- not just of good things I did but of experiences and things I overcame - help me end each year really energized about how I spent my time! I become full of positivity when I do this. I highly recommend it. If you feel prompted to do this idea, you don't have to wait until January if you are reading this later in the year. Just start today.

Another idea with a jar is to use it to give things to God. I have a Mason jar next to my bed. When something comes up that is overwhelming and so hard to cope with that I am struggling to sleep, I write that thing down on a piece of paper, tell God I am giving it to Him to worry about, and put it in the jar. As long as that paper is in the jar, I can't worry about that thing. If I want to worry about it, I must take the paper out and hold it. Then I can pass it back to God by putting it back in the jar. This exercise is very helpful for me, and if I am worried about something, I sleep a lot better at night if I remember to do this before bed.

Technology Boundaries

Every time you get that little buzz for a text, message, like, update, or anything, your brain releases dopamine. Basically, you are getting a little high from these notifications. At one point, I noticed that when I felt panicky, if I played Candy Crush I would eventually calm down as my brain focused on the game, and I got little rewards. It would take about 30 minutes of playing, but I could get out of a panic attack, as long as I didn't run out of lives too early. However I became more and more dependent on this to make me happy. I would play multiple times a day, sometimes for hours and hours, and sometimes I would get really angry if my life ran out on the game! I just wanted to play and not worry about anything else. After about eight months of this, I realized that I probably had an addiction. But I rationalized playing because it was helping me with my anxiety!

At one point, I had a mini panic attack when I was on vacation with my family. I grabbed my phone, went to a secluded location, and started to play my game. My dad noticed and came over. He wrapped his arm around me and just held me. My anxiety levels quickly went down. At that moment, I realized that there are different ways to get through my panic attacks, and that some things actually work better or faster than others. That hug was much faster working than a video game for me. I decided to delete Candy Crush from my phone. I went through some withdrawals at first, but only for about a week. After that I replaced my game with things that were more meaningful. I found that I had less anxiety when I wasn't wasting my time, and I've been able to find better ways to cope with my panic attacks.

The best way to use your phone in a positive way rather than letting it make you more anxious/depressed is to set limits. Set limits on how much time you spend on your phone. You can even download apps that set a time limit on how long you can use other apps. I do that, and although it's annoying to be cut off when I am in the middle of scrolling, I am grateful that I am not controlled by my phone as much as I could be. You can go on a fast from your phone for a while to see the difference in your life. There has never been so much technology, and so much depression. I have noticed a personal connection between social media and depression. I especially noticed this when I took President Nelson's challenge to go off of social media for 10 days a couple of years back. I felt so good, I continued the media fast for a couple extra days. I don't plan on ever getting rid of my social media since I value it for relationships and work. But when I am feeling sad, I do better if I can remember that social media doesn't help and look for other ways to cope with my emotions.

Humor

Another way to overcome anxiety is by finding humor. Try to see the funny side of things in life. People who are able to do this are much happier.

There's a woman I know and admire a lot who was single until her early 30s. She is a couple years older than me and is one of those people I admire from a distance. We went to college together and I have followed her over the years via Facebook and learned many things from her.

For a time while she was single, she went off to Alaska to be a schoolteacher. Every school day, she posted something funny that happened to her, or that she did at school. She would say, "89th Day of School" and then post something funny from that day. How was she able to come up with something for each day, year after year? She knows how to enjoy each moment and look for the humor and she brightens life for others by sharing those experiences. I really admire that ability and want to become more like her. We probably all could find something humorous about each day, but instead we get too wrapped up in our own woes and miss a lot of the good around us. Laughing is something you can do right now which helps anxiety and relieves stress!

Set Boundaries

Setting boundaries helps ease stress and anxiety. I had an experience with this during college. During my senior year, I played Fruma Sarah in *Fiddler on the Roof*. Fruma Sarah is the crazy dead lady that Tevye pretends comes to him in a dream. It's Tevye's tactic to convince his wife that their daughter should marry the man she wants to and not Fruma Sarah's widower husband.

Fruma Sarah just has one song in the show, but it's an awesome song and she's one of my all-time favorite roles. I had already done it in high school, and when we did it at my university, I already knew I could rock that role. But in call backs, they kept having me sing for one of the three daughters. After a while, I looked around to see how many girls were hoping to be picked to be one of the daughters. Being the ingenue is fun, and most girls love to be the pretty girl. I knew no one else would want to be Fruma Sarah. I also knew I could probably do that role better than anyone else. So before they had me do another sister scene for the 12th time, I asked if it would be ok if I sang the Fruma Sarah song. As soon as I was done the looks on their faces told me I got the part.

I had my part memorized by the first rehearsal. By the time we got to performances, I could do the role in my sleep. To me, the performances seemed flawless. One night I even received a standing ovation at the end of my song. However, for whatever reason, our music director felt the need to come down to my dressing room before every show or during intermissions to give me critiques and notes. This wasn't just confusing, it was debilitating. He had never given me a single instruction during rehearsals, but now that I had an audience he was coming regularly and telling me to make changes. It made me feel stupid and stressed. I talked to the show director, who simply said "he shouldn't be doing that". But he wouldn't talk to the music director.

One night I almost didn't go on stage because I was crying so hard. I was struggling with anxiety and depression at the time and didn't have much self-confidence. At last, I did go on stage, and sure enough during intermission he came down again to say I was singing too fast. That was enough! I finally said, "Look, I am just going to do it the way I practiced it ok?!" He said, "Ok", and never bothered me again. I wished I had stood up for myself sooner. I went on to have a great last couple of performances. I don't know what made him behave like that. But as soon as I set boundaries, I was ok and he didn't bother me anymore. This eased my anxiety in the situation a lot.

Keep an Eternal Perspective

One of my sisters once called me in a panic because she fell victim to a phone scam and was scared she had ruined our family's life because she given the scammer remote access to my parents' computer. Luckily, my office was only four minutes away from my parents' house so I drove there.

My sister was a mess and was devastated by what she had done. When she realized the caller was a scammer, she shut down the computer, but she was still freaking out. To calm her down, I asked, "Did what you do make it so that anyone in our family won't make it to the Celestial Kingdom?" She stopped and thought and said no. Almost instantly she was much calmer. We talked about how even if she had given the scammer information that would ruin our family financially, or caused us other problems, in the grand scheme of life, it wasn't a big deal.

Having an eternal perspective helps calm my fears. Remembering what is truly important, and that this life isn't the end, helps me stay positive, and it worked for my sister too. A testimony of the gospel of Jesus Christ truly is one of the best things for helping me overcome fears and anxieties, and I am so grateful to have these truths in my life.

There are many other fears that I didn't mention, like fear of complications with childbirth/child development by having children when you are older, fear of divorce, fear of the death of a spouse, or fear that in this life or the next we will have to live polygamy. Really the list of potential fears is endless, and you're not the first woman to have these fears. Whatever your fear, you can always choose faith. We can look to the future with hope and trust that ultimately we will have perfect joy and happiness, even if we can't see the how or when. In the Elder Dale G. Renlund talk I referenced earlier he said about Christ, "He will not just console us and restore what was lost; He will use the unfairness for our benefit." This is what I try to focus on, as I work on ever changing from a "worrier" to a "warrior" with Christ.

Alissa M.'s Story - Leçons d'être célibataire (Lessons on Being Single)

Several years ago, I was lying in bed one night reading my scriptures when I came across a beautiful story told by President Thomas S. Monson in his talk entitled, "In Search of Treasures." The story takes place in 1892 and tells of a boy named Benjamin who traveled to Salt Lake to fulfill his dream of auditioning for an orchestra. The conductor was impressed by the audition and invited him to join Fall rehearsals. Delighted, he returned home with the news and prospect of being in a prestigious orchestra. While home, Benjamin's bishop asked him to postpone his dream and instead serve a mission. Knowing that his family could not afford to pay for his mission, he counseled with his mother about what to do. Selling more of the farm was not an option, so she told him there was one way for him to raise enough money: he would have to sell his violin. Heartbroken, but filled with faith, Ben played his violin for the last time, sold it, and left on his mission. Many years later, he wrote in his journal that the best thing he'd ever done was choose to give up what he loved to the God he loved even more.

    This passage so inspired me that I found myself asking if there were things in my life or desires of my heart that I needed to surrender to God? Were there dreams and hopes and wishes that I was holding on to, bitter that they hadn't yet been realized by God's plan for me?

    It was at least six or so months later when I got married to the man that I fell in love with. As many of us dream of romance, I felt I had fallen into a beautiful love story. Shortly after we were married, however, pornography found its way back into my husband's life. His dishonesty and secrecy kept it hidden from me, and I found myself living in fear of the future. As our marriage began to crumble beneath my feet, I pleaded with the Lord to help me know how to help my husband and how to save our marriage. I soon began to learn, however, that saving our marriage was not my responsibility alone.

    I had been married for about ten months when I started to reach a breaking point. I knew and had been told that marriage wasn't supposed to be easy, but truthfully? I didn't think it would be as hard as it was. I felt confused all the time - and there were days when I didn't even understand what to think or believe anymore. I still remember the fear that overcame me when my husband mentioned how tired he was of having faith, that it was illogical and just too difficult. I wasn't against asking difficult questions and wrestling with principles that don't always make sense. And at the same time, I was terrified of what would happen if he gave up having faith.

My brain was a fog and I felt responsible for every conflict or problem that came up. Looking back, I know I was manipulated and gas lighted and emotionally abused on a regular basis, but at the time I had no idea what was going on. All I knew was that I believed I was the reason my marriage was failing. I remember one night, early on in our marriage, when my husband and I were making pizza. I was trying to figure out a way to bring up chastity, something our bishop had challenged each couple to go home and discuss. He wanted us to practice being open and honest and faithful to one another. So, as I carefully began the conversation with my husband, eventually it turned to what he thought I was lacking - particularly self-confidence. He wanted to help me gain more self-esteem and a higher sense of self-worth, and so the discussion that I wanted to have with him about pornography and fidelity never happened. Instead, the conversation shifted to my weakness of self-esteem and how I needed to learn to love myself. While it was true, I did need to learn to love and think higher of myself, I couldn't figure out how the conversation turned away from fidelity in our marriage to him being concerned about my low self-esteem.

Several weeks later, I found out that he had relapsed - and had been relapsing - for about three weeks, yet he had chosen to keep it a secret. After I put two and two together, I realized how inspired our bishop had been when he had invited us to counsel together as couples concerning chastity and keeping our marriages free from dishonesty and secrecy. My heart was broken, and I tore myself down, wondering above all things, what I needed to change about myself in order for him to feel comfortable talking to me. I believed that I was the one who was most flawed and was the reason for the ever-growing distance between us.

If you were to ask me at what point our marriage started to weaken, I don't know that I could tell you. But what I can tell you is that throughout the process of being single, married, and then divorced, one of the most important truths I learned was that surrendering my will to God's brought me closer to Him - and my Heavenly Mother - than I ever thought possible. And I truly started learning how to do this when Heavenly Father blessed me with a life coach.

One day, a neighbor noticed me leave my house in tears. She texted me later, asked if I was alright, and upon finding out that I was not in a good emotional state, gave me the contact information for our Bishop's wife who happened to be a life coach. I didn't have enough money at the time to pay for coaching, so I put the information on the backburner and hoped I'd never have to talk to someone. Unfortunately, I felt ashamed to ask for help, and I felt burdened to keep my husband's addiction a secret from everyone. It weighed on my shoulders so heavily that it occupied my mind more than I can even describe. Yet still I hoped I could fix my marriage on my own.

Several months went by and I came to the realization that fixing my marriage wasn't really up to me. In fact, I was powerless. During those several months, the darkness I felt was overwhelmingly deep and I was at the end of my rope. That's when I decided to pull out the information my neighbor had given me and call our Bishop's wife. My hands shook as I picked up my car keys and snuck out of the house. I didn't think my husband would notice that I was gone, so I didn't bother telling him I was leaving for a bit. I got into my little car and drove to a location where I felt safe and alone. I carefully dialed the number I had been given nearly three months previously, and then I waited.

She didn't pick up and so I decided to leave a message that went something like this: "Hi Sister Cambell (name changed), it's Alissa. I was told by a ward member that you are a life coach and that you would be willing to take on another client. I don't have the money to pay you right now, but I will once I get a job. I just really need some help with my marriage...I don't know what to do." And with that, my voice cracked, and I hung up the phone just as sobs of fear, despair and utter loneliness left my body. I had no other solutions to what was going on – she was my only idea, my only possible way to survive. My body slumped against the seat, and I laid my head on my steering wheel, ready to admit defeat.

And then?

A tiny ray of sunlight came through the window and warmed my face. Instantly, I knew that God was there beside me - and there He would stay. He just needed me to hold on a little longer by trusting Him and surrendering my will. I knew that somehow and, in some way, He could work a miracle, whatever that miracle would turn out to be.

I don't remember at what time that day she called back, but it wasn't long after I had returned home that she returned my call. I cried so much those first few phone calls - the destitution I felt was nearly tangible. I was confused. Lost. In the dark. Worried. Heart-broken. Lonely. And not sure if my marriage would last.

One of the very first truths my life coach taught me was that I mattered, and my feelings mattered. Just because my husband wasn't able to hear me and see me for what I was feeling didn't mean that I wasn't lovable. I *was* lovable and I *did* have worth. A second vital truth she taught me was that I am not responsible for how someone else decides to act. I alone control my own actions and reactions. Thus, the way my husband chose to react to what I said or did was his responsibility and his alone.

If I could go back to my pre-married self, back to that twenty-four-year-old woman who was falling in love with a handsome, tall and genuinely good young man; back to that girl who believed she was not good enough; back to that young woman who looked outward for approval and acceptance; if I could go back to my pre-married self, I would wrap her in my arms, remind her that she was important, and that nothing and no one could touch her worth. She was enough - no matter what the media or her grades or the adversary or the popular crowd said. She was already enough. And then I would let her know that she was free to live her dreams regardless of the opinions of those around her. She had permission to be who she was and where she was.

Personal Peace

Thanks to my life coach, I learned tools which helped me identify moments when I was self-denigrating and believing that I wasn't enough. I learned how to identify manipulation and how to stand up for myself and for my safety. As I learned these tools, I wished I could go back in time to the beginning of my marriage and give myself a hug whenever I was blaming myself and taking responsibility for my husband's actions. As I learned to set boundaries, I began to teach myself that I was important, that my safety mattered, and that I was and always would be enough.

I didn't always have these tools though, and I often fell victim to abuse and manipulation. One night in particular, about ten months into my marriage, stands out in my mind. My husband and I were taking a carload of belongings from our old apartment to a new one where we would stay until he got accepted to grad school. That night, I sat silently and nervously in the car as we drove, my heart weeping because I felt terrified to talk to him. Earlier, we'd had a tense argument, and I felt like everything was my fault and that I was responsible for fixing it. I usually told myself that I needed to be the one apologizing and taking the blame.

As we pulled into the driveway of the new place, he put the car in park and made a motion for me to not open the door just yet. He placed his left hand on the steering wheel and turned towards me, though I dared not look back. Instead, I sat in shock, staring at the ground as I heard him say that he wished I looked like a supermodel and would wear more makeup in order to look beautiful. After encouraging me to exercise more so as to be more sexually attractive to him, he ended by saying these words: "But you're what I've got, so I'll just have to deal with it."

I was speechless. Frozen in place. *Is this really my husband talking to me?*

I look back on that moment and watch my small, barely one-hundred-pound self invisibly shrink into a ball and weep. And I weep with her. I wrap my arms around her and whisper, "You are not responsible for how he is acting, and you are enough. You are always enough." Truthfully, the worst part of this memory is not what he said to me. The worst part is that I believed him. Yes, his words were hurtful, and it was emotionally abusive to treat his wife in this way. And at the same time, I believed him. I believed that I wasn't good enough for him; that I was flawed and feeble. I let his words crush me.

Now that I am divorced and have spent nearly two years working with my life coach, those two truths that I learned through my experiences have truly changed my life: 1) I matter and my feelings matter, and 2) I am never responsible for some else's actions.

As a single woman again, I have had to discover how to reintegrate myself into the young single adult life. For the first several months after my divorce, I felt that I was walking around with a giant sign on my head that read, "I'm divorced". I felt like an outcast. But I learned to apply the truth that it didn't matter what others thought of me. I am who I am. I am enough. God knows what I have been through, and for me, that is sufficient. My worth is not defined by my marital status - nor my divorced status, and besides, I would never trade my past for anything because I am grateful for what I have learned.

Words that saved me.

For a long time, the poem had no title, but as I read it throughout the months that followed its completion, I soon felt to entitle it *Surrender* because by surrendering my will to God's, I have learned more about myself, my Saviour, and my Heavenly Parents than I ever thought possible.

Surrender.

I fall to my knees at the end of the day,
The tears leave my eyes, and I have nothing to say.
I feel overcome by the darkness inside.
It tortures my spirit, and I just want to hide.

Personal Peace

My heart has been torn and it won't seem to heal,
And I long for the happiness that I used to feel.

I question my faith as I kneel by my bed:
Do I truly believe Christ will do as He said?
This pain overwhelms me and aches in my soul!
Do I truly believe Christ can make my heart whole?

How can I let go of the things I hold dear,
How can I give place for faith over fear?
When the future is dim and I can't see the light,
How can I keep walking when I'm afraid of the night?

The Truth is that sometimes we experience pain
because that is the only way to obtain
The joy and the happiness we were sent here to have -
Amidst all our anguish and days that are sad.

Though cry as we will, God numbers our tears.
He answers our prayers and he quiets our fears.
Quite simply the truth is in order to feel
The love He extends for our hearts to heal,
To Him our will we must surrender up,
And sometimes must drink from the small bitter cup.

But He promises blessings and joy through the tears,
So I'll continue to trust and believe that he hears
The pleas of my heart, though weak I may be.
He won't leave me comfortless - He will come unto me.

Quietly, gently, peace comforts my soul
And beside me I picture my loving Saviour.
As I choose to act in the way that Christ did,
As I say what He'd say and live as He lived,
I cannot completely partake of God's gift

Overcoming Fears

Until I have given the one thing to give.

My desires and passions, though right they may be,
Are nothing compared to what God wants for me.
As I freely will choose to follow His son;
I'll give him my will so that we can be one.
His purpose, my purpose, His will is now mine,
He knows he can trust me with errands divine.

So here is my faith, my desires, my dreams.
I'll give them to thee, though hard it may seem.
I'll give what I love and the life I adore,
Surrender my will to the God I love more.

- Alissa M

    To the single women who struggle not knowing whether or not the future will bring a marriage and a family, I would say to remember the story of the young man and his violin. Trust that you can surrender your will. Surrender the outcomes of the future and the outcomes of other people's actions and embrace the truth that God will take care of your future for you.

Chapter 12
Finding Hope

"There may be times when we must make a courageous decision to hope even when everything around us contradicts that hope... We learn to cultivate hope the same way we learn to walk, one step at a time." - "The Infinite Power of Hope", Dieter F. Uchtdorf, *Ensign*, November 2008

Sadness

Many single women have this thought: *I wouldn't feel sad if I were married.* I used to think that if I was married with kids, I wouldn't be so sad and feel like life was so pointless. If only I had kids, then I would have a reason to live. But I have learned that is not how God sees things. Maybe when I do get married, those feelings I have at times of having a pointless existence won't suddenly go away. Perhaps they are not connected to a future family, but Satan wants me to think that so I will stay sad, instead of being grateful for what I have. I have learned it's important to work on being happy now and finding peace and joy today.

Remember that no matter how bad it gets, every emotion is temporary. The sun will shine again. Many of the things I discuss in this book are things I tried so that I didn't have to feel like my life was pointless. I had to give myself purpose, direction, and motivation. Sometimes I have felt unqualified to write this book, because I am an example of *every* negative thing I have written about. I have had so many days where I struggled to want to try, struggled to have faith for one more day. But even though I have had so many terrible days, full of anxiety and depression, I still keep trying again the next day. Sometimes that is my reason for living, to keep trying to find a point to it all. Falling and failing gives me more to write about. And hoping that I can help someone else on their journey who is struggling with something similar is great motivation to continue with this book.

God doesn't want you to see your gift of life as meaningless. The cure to sorrow is not marriage. It never has been and never will be, no matter how many Romantic Comedies you watch. The good news is that there is a cure, and that is Jesus Christ. Because we are in a fallen world, things will never be perfect. However, little by little I have gained a testimony that as we turn to Him, we can have peace and hope even when things seem impossibly hard. He has led me to learn many things about my sorrows, and how to overcome them. This chapter is about those things.

Overcoming

Depression can come for different reasons. It can be situational- meaning you become depressed because of external events, or it can be connected to your health- a chemical imbalance. It can also be a choice- a neurological pathway that is selected repeatedly until it becomes a habitual response to things that happen. I have struggled with all three of these versions of depression.

To start tackling this issue, you must make depression real, make it tangible. Think of it like a broken arm. When your arm breaks, you go to the hospital. There are doctors and nurses there to help you. When you push a button, you get pain medicine. When I was going through some of my hardest times, my dad told me to make him my 'nurse'. If I was going into a panic attack, or a major bout of depression, I would call him. This was like my button for the nurse to come and check on me; my dad was one of my nurses. We also had a family friend who I will call Kellie, who has dealt with depression all her life who was another "nurse" of mine. I would call her, and she would have me talk things through with her.

This really helped. It made me feel like this was not just me 'overreacting'. It was an actual problem, and I was able to get help when I needed it. It took my dad a while to understand that I really did have a problem. It took learning how to explain what I was experiencing. It took moments of me figuring out the difference- when I was in my right mind versus when I was in panic mode/depressed mode.

Once when I was in that intense mode, I happened to be at my parents' house. My parents sat with me and talked to me as I cried. As I talked to them, the panic and confusion subsided. There was a shift in me that they were able to see. That helped my dad change his view on the issue, and he became my biggest ally from then on. My mom also helped by finding emotional tools to help me as well as supplements. We treated this as a real issue, and that really helped. I did have to learn how to communicate about it though. I had to really work at explaining what I was dealing with and seeing the difference. It was hard to think that maybe this was going to be something I would have to deal with my whole life. I worried that I was going to be in and out of my panic/depressed state until the Resurrection. So, I decided I was going to figure out how to cope with it.

Notice It

Notice when it is starting. This is one thing that Kellie and later my therapist helped me to do. Kellie told me to watch for the patterns and notice when you start to react and go into a panic or depression. This was huge for me. When you learn to recognize the beginning of the downward spiral, it is much easier to turn it around. The first few times I realized that I was starting to enter the panic zone was when driving. I would be driving home from work, and if something made me nervous, like a car honking at me or making a lane change, it could really set me off. Without realizing it I would start breathing faster and heavier. I would then start thinking about how terrible of a driver I was. I would start thinking about how dangerous and scary driving is! And then I would start worrying and apologizing to all the cars around me for my driving. I'd feel terrified that I would make a mistake. The next thing you know I would be in a hopeless panic.

    I told Kellie this. She told me to focus on my breathing the next time I started to feel the anxiety start up- keep it slow and regular. A new opportunity came up quickly- I accidentally cut someone off the next day. Luckily they didn't honk at me (honking instantly made me panic). But I noticed that my breathing pattern started to change. So, I focused on that. I started taking deep breaths. I told myself that everything was ok, and a few minutes later, I felt better! I did not go into anxiety mode and I was ok! I was so amazed and relieved. It wasn't that hard and I was able to do it. Within a few months I got to the point where I felt like a normal person driving. If I could catch it as it was starting, I was much more likely to overcome it and not sink so low or so dark. It took me a couple of years of working on this, but now years later I no longer have any fear of driving. In fact, if I didn't journal about these experiences, I probably would have forgotten just how bad it used to be!

Track It

    Are you always depressed around the same time of the month? Start keeping track in a journal. Depression can come because of a chemical imbalance. As I started tracking mine, I found there were patterns. Events or experiences could make it go crazy high, but it tended to be better and worse consistently at certain times of the month, typically the week before my period. So, I talked to nutritionists and medical specialists and found that this was probably due to my body struggling to absorb B vitamins. I started taking B6 and B12 mix-in-your-drink supplements and it totally helped! It took me a while to notice the difference, but when I was able to keep my head above water emotionally for a month, I realized it worked! That was a big help: just learning that I actually have a physical disability that is making it very difficult to stay happy like a 'normal' person. I treated it as a medical condition, the same as a cold or broken bone.

Here is a tip if the depression you have is related to your physical make up: eat less sugar. I know when I eat a lot of sugar, it throws my emotions out of whack. A psychologist told me that if you do eat sugar (since totally going without is no fun), just make sure to eat protein near the same time to help break up the sugars better in the body.

Don't Seek It Out

Sometimes sadness becomes a habit, or an addiction. This happened to me. I found that sometimes I really *liked* to be depressed. For a long time, I didn't realize that I liked it, but therapy helped me see that I actually got some enjoyment out of pitying myself. Panicking was scary- I never liked reaching that point. But sadness made me feel like I could feel things deeply, which I liked. It made my prayers seem so much better and deeper and stronger if I could cry them out. When I didn't cry while praying, I felt like maybe I wasn't praying with all my heart or real intent. Essentially, I invited the depression in. This made overcoming depression harder, because I enjoyed it sometimes. I had to seek the rewards of real happiness, by choosing to give up the smaller enjoyment of self-pity and sadness. This was harder to change and took little changes over two years of therapy, but eventually I succeeded.

If you can relate to that a bit, the solution might be to change your thought patterns. I remember the night I finally decided to choose happiness over sadness. I had just laid in bed when I started to think about something super depressing. But I stopped myself and said, "No, you don't have to think about that! You can think about something else!" And I did. I thought about positive things that happened during that day and after just a few minutes, I wasn't sad. I was happy and I went right to sleep! It wasn't always that easy; overcoming this issue took time. But I am so grateful that I have made so much progress, because now my bad days are rare and my good days are common. Note that this is not because I am in a relationship- this all has to do with just me.

Push Ahead

It is important that you figure out your own coping mechanisms now so that you are ready to deal with stress, depression, and anxiety at all times of life. One thing Satan has tried to tell me is, "How could you be a mom? Your depression will only ruin kids". I have many friends whose parents have emotional challenges including depression. As a result, they grew up with a better understanding and awareness about mental health. Sometimes they learned great skills for what *not* to do, but ultimately they turned out to be great people even though their moms struggled. Depression will not stop you from being a fantastic mom. But you can work on healthy ways to deal with it. God *gives* us weaknesses (Ether 12:27). They are gifts. But then He also provides the way for us to do all that He wants us to do despite these gifts of weakness (1 Ne 3:7). I have total confidence that eventually my emotional weaknesses will become strengths. I have already seen benefits in my life as I work on overcoming the difficulties that come with these gifts from God. I am closer to God because of my struggles. If only for that, it's worth it. God is more interested in our salvation than our comfort. If 'all' I get out of my depression and anxiety is a seat in the Kingdom of God, I will be forever grateful for it.

Do it even when you don't feel like it

Find things that make you happy and make a list of those things. Post it on your wall. When you are depressed, look at this list and do one of these things. You will not want to. But do it anyway. Here's the reality. You're never going to *feel* like doing any self-help things when you are depressed. When you are depressed, the most you feel like doing is pressing a button on your phone or TV remote. You have to make yourself do things when you don't want to. That may sound wrong, but it is how it works with any sickness or injury. You have to do some things that are painful or difficult in order to heal.

    About a month into being a foster mom, my daughter sprained her ankle. In my experience, you always ice a sprain to bring down the swelling. This was terrifying to her and she did not want to do it. I had to show her articles on Google to prove to her that this was what she should do, and confirm with my mom before she agreed to try it. I ran to the store, bought a ton of ice, brought it back and made an ice bath for her foot. She was really strong, and did this three times a day for three days. We also wrapped it and rubbed Icy Hot on it. None of these things were fun, and she didn't enjoy not being able to skateboard, but she healed quickly and was fine after.

    A couple weeks after this event, I had a morning where I was really struggling with depression. I dropped my foster daughter off at school, and was laying on the couch, trying to read scriptures. I took two little naps, and still couldn't get myself up. I had planned to go on a run that morning, but that was the last thing I wanted to do now!

    Then I remembered the ice baths. My foster daughter had not wanted to do that. She was terrified of it. And yet, I knew it was going to be the best thing to help her, and the swelling would improve a lot if she did it. The spirit seemed to bring that to my mind as if to say: a sprained ankle and depression are not so different. Both hurt, but both can be overcome if you are willing to do things that help. I realized that for me, running for depression was like icing a sprained ankle. You absolutely don't want to do it, but it's what will help the problem. So, I forced myself to get off that couch and got into exercise clothes. I still didn't want to go, but I was already feeling proud of myself for getting off the couch. I knew I could do this, just like my daughter had done the ice foot bath. I went out on the run. Somewhere during that run, I did start to feel better. By the time I got home I was in a much better place emotionally. I am very grateful the spirit taught me that important lesson about depression that day.

Finding Hope

Exercise

Exercise is one of the most powerful and immediate ways to get a mood boost. Running, yoga, or pretty much any body movements help- even 10 seconds of jumping jacks. And yes, it is the last thing you will want to do. So just picture a doctor coming to you and saying, "looks like we have a case of depression. The prescribed method to cure this bout of depression is a healthy run today. And it looks like you will need to do that daily for the next couple of weeks." If a doctor tells you to take a nasty medicine, or do chemotherapy, or any of the other horrible things doctors say you have to do, you do it, because it heals you. Think about it like that if you have to.

Exercise, despite how much I still struggle to make myself do it some days, is definitely one of the top things I do for depression. Running is the exercise that gets me the best and quickest happiness buzz. The longer I run, the better I feel, too. At first, I would run and walk for just a mile. It took me at least six months to move past a mile, and to keep a steady jog that whole time.

Then I had a friend invite me to do a half marathon with her. I said, "no way!" But it planted a seed. I started thinking that maybe I couldn't do a half marathon, but why not work up to a 5k? So that's what I did. When I ran my first three miles, I was very proud of myself, and felt happy not just from having run, but also for accomplishing something I didn't think I could do.

The next year, my friend convinced me to do the half marathon with her. Each Saturday I would add another mile to my run, switching off between walking and jogging. But I did it every week, no matter how much I didn't *feel* like doing it when I woke up. Every single time afterwards, I was so glad I did it. Feelings are such interesting things. Something I have learned from successful entrepreneurs is to do things based upon who you *are*, not how you *feel*. This applies to me with running. I do it because I want to be healthy emotionally and because I have the goal of doing the half marathon and I am a person who accomplishes goals. The majority of the time, I do not run because I feel like running.

Eventually the day of the half marathon (13 mile) race came. The race was in Moab Utah, with the red rocks on one side and the Green River on the other. Crossing that finish line was one of the happiest moments of my life. That happy high continued for weeks. It was such an accomplishment for me, and I could hardly believe I'd actually done it. Mentally and emotionally, I felt incredible. Even years later, when my therapist had me think of a time when I was exhausted yet happy, I thought of finishing that 13-mile race.

I have now run three half marathons. I keep doing them because the motivation to run is still not super strong, but having that goal with a specific end date and reason to run helps a lot. There have been struggles for sure. I have learned I need to buy new running shoes each year and wear knee braces every time I run. I also need to have a good sports bra or my shoulders and back can hurt. And after finishing that first race, I learned the importance of really stretching out well afterwards. But the mental and emotional boost I get keep me coming back to running year after year.

Get Enough Rest

When it comes down to it, sometimes you just need what I call "recovery days". They are the days when you just have to let go and not do anything. You have to be careful not to allow too much recovery time - you've got to beat depression. But sometimes that won't happen without a day or two of just being a vegetable. A day or two where you give yourself permission not to put your all into your work that day, where you just get by with the minimum, can be really helpful. Some people, when they get depressed, go into minimum mode and they stay there a long time. Part of the reason for this is that they never give themselves permission to be in that place. Guilt is a terrible motivator- just think about when you try to lose weight. Love is much more powerful. Love says it's ok to take a day or two to recover. Just like a broken bone wouldn't allow you to do all you do in a regular day, being emotionally wounded needs healing time too. Love yourself. Allow yourself that recovery time, and then get back up again.

There was a time where I was super overwhelmed, stressed, struggling, and emotional. My sister came over and patiently listened to me while I cried about everything going on. She then said, "are you getting enough sleep?" I thought about it and realized because of everything I was trying to do, I had been getting less sleep. I went and took a 20-minute nap and I was so much happier! I made sure I got more sleep that night, and the next morning, I was doing great.

Feed Your Spirit

Caring for your physical body is important in battling depression, and so is caring for your spirit. You can turn to the scriptures to feed your spirit. The more I have studied the scriptures while doing therapy, the more I have realized God does give us the tools to combat things like depression and anxiety. "Let Virtue garnish thy thoughts unceasingly." (D&C 121:45) When I was in Young Women's, I thought this scripture was just about bad or dirty thoughts. But now that I know that depression comes from dwelling on sad and upsetting ideas and thoughts, this scripture tells me what to do to overcome depression.

A scripture that I have come to love is "take therefore no thought for the morrow, for the morrow shall take thought for the things of itself." (3 Ne 13:33) Anxiety means you constantly focus on what could happen and the what-if scenarios. In this scripture, God tells us to not worry in this way. It took therapy to be able to recognize what these scriptures mean to me, and now I see the scriptures as one of my tools for emotional well-being.

Connect with Others

Connecting with things and people outside yourself is an important part of batting depression. I have found it helpful to do things where someone or something else is dependent on me. One way I did this at a particularly low time in my life was by planting a garden. As soon as I bought my first eight starter plants, I felt like there were lives that depended on me. Sure, they weren't human lives, or even pets. But I learned quickly how dependent these little plants were on me. They were watered when I got them, and I intended to plant them right away, but things came up. Three days later, they were still not planted and were already starting to wilt- some of them badly! I felt like a terrible mother. I quickly went to plant them even though it was 9:00 at night. I planted them in a nice garden area, and I watered them, but I was really worried they might die! I prayed over them, and I thought about them a lot. I read more about gardening and learned how to better care for them.

I really, really wanted my garden to live. And somehow, that sense of responsibility or nurturing or whatever it was helped me have a reason to live. If I didn't get up one day, I knew none of my roommates were going to take care of my garden. My little baby plants were 100% dependent on me. And even though it wasn't as easy as I thought it was going to be, it gave me some purpose when I was struggling to find purpose.

If you have a hobby or talent, join a group of other people to practice and share that skill. Becoming part of a group that needs you and depends on you is a great way to connect with others and help with depression. For a number of years, I was in an *a cappella* group. I did not imagine when I auditioned that this group would come as a blessing because I would feel *needed* by them. The idea that they depended on me helped me feel needed and also gave me a purpose.

Get into this Moment

Singing always helps me focus on the current moment, which is very helpful for anxiety and depression. When I am singing and practicing, I am able to let go of everything else going on when I am rehearsing. I had a high school choir teacher teach us that when we are singing, we should not think about anything else. He would have us pretend to suck all of our worries out of our minds, crumple them all up into a ball, and throw them to the front door of the classroom. He would say that as soon as class was over, we could go out the door and pick up our worries again. But in a rehearsal, it is detrimental to your practice to worry about those things. I took that to heart, and I have applied that to every music rehearsal of my life. When I start to sing, that is my entire focus for that moment. When you are in the moment, you aren't thinking about the past or future: you are totally in the now.

There are other techniques to help a person come right into the present moment- physical movement works, as well as focusing on your breath. But singing also creates positive endorphins. You can feel a lot better just by singing around the house or in your car or anything! I had heard this, but I really noticed it when driving home after two-hour *a cappella* rehearsals- that laser-focus on singing would make me so happy, sometimes I would just smile and laugh the whole one-hour car ride home!

Effort is Sometimes Better Than Efficiency

I've found that depression can be worse when life becomes too convenient. Our society is focused on being as efficient as possible so we have more time to do what we want. This sounds good, in theory. But then sometimes you don't know what to do with that extra time. We cut corners and spend money to save time, but what are we doing with that time?

I went through a phase where I realized that while I had more time to do what I wanted, instead of developing hobbies or volunteering at charities, I was spending tons of time on social media and was not happy. One day as I was driving, I realized that I really needed to wash my car. I was thinking about what kind of wash I wanted to spend my money on, a basic one, or a more advanced one that would be more expensive. I didn't really want to spend a bunch of money on a car wash... but it's good to have a clean car, I reasoned.

As my mind dwelt on this, I thought about the cost to hand wash my car. I reasoned that while it would be cheaper, it would also be a huge waste of time. But then I thought about the benefits of washing my car myself. I would save money on the car wash, but I would also get a little exercise as well. And I'd save gas and miles driving to and through a car wash. It wouldn't be a huge savings, but it might be good practice at saving in tiny areas. Little things, compounded over time, make a difference.

So, one Saturday, I decided to buy car washing supplies while I was out shopping with my roommate. She was talking about how she needed to wash her car too. So I bought her and I both a sponge and some soap, all for under $10. Then we got in our swimsuits, blasted some music, and washed our cars.

It was...fun! On top of saving money and getting in some body movement, we had fun together. And I had car wash supplies to last me all summer! The only thing I forgot was an old towel to dry the car with, but luckily my roommate had one for us to use. We also got a good dose of Vitamin D. If I had gone through the car wash, I would only have saved 15-20 minutes in time. Washing my car by hand saved me money, burned calories, gave me a good time, and even worked my tan. Sometimes we try to make life so convenient that we miss out on things that make us feel better.

Be Grateful

Being grateful can be a game changer if you are depressed. The first time I used gratitude to overcome depression was in high school. I was in church and we sang the song "Count your Many Blessings". Verse 4 really stood out to me:

4. So amid the conflict, whether great or small,
Do not be discouraged; God is over all.
Count your many blessings; angels will attend,
Help and comfort give you to your journey's end.

Finding Hope

After hearing and reading those lyrics, I sat down with a notebook and pen that week, and started writing down things I had that I was grateful for. I could hardly believe how quickly I started to feel better! It was amazing! I don't know why it's so easy to become ungrateful, living in this amazing and beautiful country, at a time when we have more than anyone in the history of the earth. Yet somehow the plague of ingratitude is everywhere. I definitely struggle with this. But when I make an effort to be grateful, life isn't so bad.

During my last year of college, sometimes I would get so depressed I would climb under my bed, curl up and try to disappear. I really wanted to get out of my funk, and inspiration came from the Holy Ghost telling me to be grateful. Because of that, every night before bed I would write something I was grateful for that day on a quarter sheet of different-colored paper and tape it to my wall. As something was added each day, it was easy to see how many blessings I had! My roommates and friends had fun trying to make it onto my wall too. It brightened my room, and I felt better with all those blessings looking at me. It was still a hard semester- but being grateful was a huge help to me making it through it.

There are things to be grateful for specifically as a single person. I see married friends complaining on social media about trying to figure out what to make for dinner, and having to do that for the next 60 years of their lives. Sometimes I struggle to decide what to do for dinner, but I don't have other people depending on me to figure that out by a certain time. Sometimes I just snack as I think about what to make for dinner and then I am full. Or I decide to eat some ice cream at 6:00 and later eat a meal when I feel like it… or just more ice cream. I am grateful that I am not 'trapped' in the dinner cycle. Maybe you are really looking forward to that, but there are other things unique to the single life that you can find and be grateful for. There are perks to being single. Choosing to be happy now makes me feel good.

Repentance

God might tell us something we need to do to change that is hard to hear, and that we don't want to do. Or, maybe we don't even know we have an issue or problem. We come to God like in Ether 12:27 to ask God about our weaknesses. As He promises, God will show us our weaknesses. Because we sometimes wish we were already perfect, or we expect ourselves to be perfect, we dislike feedback from others or God. Realizing that you are not perfect can be hard, because it means you've got to admit that and then do something about it.

When I let go of pride, and truly humble myself, and commit myself to do whatever God says that I need to improve, repentance starts to become sweet to me. I'm sitting there running into the wall over and over and over again. Finally, I talk about it with God. Or oftentimes His answers will come to me through a friend or family member. I talk about my problems, and then God's solution appears. I realize what I have been trying to do and why it isn't working. And it's because I haven't been doing what God says. He points this out to me and it stings a little at first. But then, it's *awesome*! Now I don't have to keep running into a wall, I understand why that wall is there- I built it! I can change by breaking it down or going around it. That is what repentance is- the change and sweet relief that comes from it. I am now much more grateful for those breakthroughs or realizations of what I was doing wrong. Repentance is that process, and it makes me better and life sweeter.

Stop Beating Yourself Up

Although there are many helpful techniques to fight depression, the most important is this: stop beating yourself up when you make a mistake. Remember that one of the main reasons we are here on this earth is to gain experience. God *expects* us to make mistakes. That is why He provided the atonement of His son, Jesus Christ; it covers every sin, mistake, or weakness. If you struggle with this idea, say it often to yourself: "We are meant to gain experience. We are expected to make mistakes."

I once went to an LDS Addiction Recovery group for Women. It was an extremely spiritual experience. And the best thing I took away from that class was right at the end, when one of the Senior Sister missionaries said, "every time you try it's a win". You don't fail if you have doubts. You don't fail if you struggle with a sin. You don't fail at anything, as long as you try again.

In the talk "Repentance Is Always Positive" by Stephen W. Owen, he talks about the prodigal son. When this son finally decided that he would go home to his father after wasting away all his inheritance, he had to walk. Brother Owen said, "I've often wondered about the son's long walk home. Were there times when he hesitated and wondered, 'How will I be received by my father?' Perhaps he even took a few steps back toward the swine. Imagine how the story would be different if he had given up. But faith kept him moving…" One thing I have learned from studying addictions: If you don't like yourself, it is much harder to make changes. When I finally accepted my body, and chose to start calling myself healthy, I started losing the inches and pounds I always wanted to. I originally thought shaming and guilting myself would make me change, but it didn't. It was loving myself enough to want to take care of myself that worked. When you mess up, give yourself a hug. You *lived!* You took a risk and a chance. If you never want that to happen again, forgive yourself and love yourself even if you keep making the same mistake for a while- even a long while. God will give you time to overcome all your trials and weaknesses. You are not the first or the last person to wish they could be fixed right now. But perfection is a long process. Enjoy the journey, and find peace knowing that making mistakes is part of the plan, as long as we keep trying.

An awesome quote by Marjorie Hinckley says:

> I don't want to drive up to the pearly gates in a shiny sports car, wearing beautifully

tailored clothes, my hair expertly coiffed, and with long, perfectly manicured fingernails. I want to drive up in a station wagon that has mud on the wheels from taking kids to scout camp. I want to be there with a smudge of peanut butter on my shirt from making sandwiches for a sick neighbors' children. I want to be there with a little dirt under my fingernails from helping to weed someone's garden. I want to be there with children's sticky kisses on my cheeks and the tears of a friend on my shoulder. I want the Lord to know I was really here and that I really lived.

Avoid Becoming Bitter

When life is hard for long periods of time, some people become bitter. In the Book of Mormon after the many war chapters, it says some people became bitter or hardened. Alma 62:41 says, "...behold, because of the exceedingly great length of the war between the Nephites and the Lamanites many had become hardened, because of the exceedingly great length of the war..."

Becoming bitter is definitely a temptation for women of the church who expected to be married by 'now', whenever 'now' is for them. Even among women who have done everything right- the unfairness of the situation can eat away at us if we let it. Unfortunately, I sometimes see it a little in myself. My roommate and I were watching our Young Adult Stake Conference from home one Sunday during the COVID-19 Pandemic. The stake president made a comment about how he couldn't have done something without his wife. We both started sarcastically yelling at the TV, things like, "Wow, how blessed and wonderful you must be, President, to deserve a wife in life to get through trials!" It was really funny that we both did it at the same time, and of course we wouldn't have done that if we were in the chapel. But it made me think… Even though we were being funny, there was a tiny seed of bitterness inside of me.

The good news is, I don't have to water that seed of bitterness. Instead, I can let my heart be softened because of my trials. The same verse in Alma mentioned above goes on to say: "…and many were softened because of their afflictions, insomuch that they did humble themselves before God, even in the depth of humility". All the people experienced the same war. Some became hardened, others were softened. We get to pick which seeds we water and what traits we develop.

It helps me to remember there is no timeline for discipleship. It requires enduring to the end and not conditioning our actions or attitudes on God meeting our expectations in our timeframe. I know I am getting married in this life. *But if not*, I still choose to follow my Lord, and trust that His plan for me is better than mine.

Love and Hope

The opposite of depression and fear are love and hope. One of my very favorite talks ever was given by President Uchtdorf in the October 2008 Conference. I think it's the talk I've reread more than any other in my life. It's called, "The Infinite Power of Hope". Understanding hope helps me to know how to better be happy now. In that talk, the line, "we have the responsibility to make (hope) an active part of our lives and overcome the temptation to lose hope" hits me hard. It is a temptation to be sad. But that also means that sadness is something that can be overcome! I don't have to just deal with it.

After all the work I've put into overcoming depression, do I still get depressed?
Yes. Just a couple of days ago I woke up in the morning, and instead of feeling well rested and ready for a new day, I was already bawling because I am single. Waking up depressed is the worst! But because I have learned coping skills, I prayed. I told myself that it was ok I was feeling this way right now, but that it was a temporary

feeling that wouldn't last long. I took a chewable Vitamin B12 tablet. I did my morning exercise and scripture study. I took a long hot shower while breathing in lavender essential oil, and by the time it was 10am, I was feeling great.

If I can master the skill of choosing happiness now, I'll be more prepared for other things that come my way in life. I can follow Joseph B. Wirthlin's counsel to "Come what may and love it", from his last conference address before he passed away. It takes faith to have hope. That's something huge I have learned. It takes faith to believe that it will work out in the end- to have *hope* that it will work out in the end. And if it takes my whole life to develop sufficient faith in hope to be truly happy, it will all have been worth it.

Jane O.'s Story

When I was eighteen my mom gave me life-long advice. I had just graduated from high school and was frustrated. I was frustrated that I would be the only member in my family not to get into BYU. I was frustrated that people who I felt had lived a less "religious" life than I had, were receiving blessings that I wanted. I felt alone and forgotten. As I expressed my frustrations to my mom, she turned to me and said, "Don't feel sorry for yourself." This was not what I wanted to hear. I felt justified in my frustrations and felt like no one could really "understand" what I was going through. She went on to explain how when we feel sorry for ourselves we are giving into Satan. We are letting Satan tell us that Heavenly Father isn't doing enough for us, and we deserve more. In other words, we are ungrateful.

This was not an easy concept for me to apply, and it took me years to fully live it. It started with the simple reminder anytime I started to feel depressed. I would start feeling sad and had to say it out loud-- "Don't feel sorry for yourself." Sometimes that worked, but more often than not, I had to count the blessings that Heavenly Father gave me. Sometimes it only took me thinking of 3 or 4 things I was grateful for to get me out of my slump, but other times it was 20-30 things. After years of practicing gratitude "Don't feel sorry for yourself" is all I need to say to realize I am truly blessed. After years and years of choosing to be grateful it has changed me, and very seldom do I not feel grateful and I rarely get discouraged.

This does not mean that I'm never sad, or that I don't feel the pain of being single. Of course I do. I feel it every time I'm asked to do things because I'm "single". I feel it every time someone asks me if I'm dating someone. I feel it at every family party, bridal shower and baby shower I attend. I even feel it when I'm grocery shopping for myself and realize that I have no one to cook for, so I'll just buy some cereal… and maybe some ice cream! Of course I know it can be painful to be single. Of course I want to be married and have children of my own. But I will not let the fact that I'm single destroy my life. I refuse to let it. I choose to be grateful.

Instead of focusing on the life I'm missing out on, I choose to focus on the life I have. I have chosen a career I love and feel like I am making a difference in my students' lives. I have created relationships with my family members and have worked hard to become the "favorite aunt". I'm not only close to my nieces and nephews, but have become even closer to my siblings and parents. I have been in positions to serve my family and close friends when needed. I am more independent and feel stronger about my purpose in life. I have left my comfort zone and traveled the world. Most importantly, I have come to peace with who I am and have come to know Christ better and trust in His plan for me -- and that is what I am most grateful for.

Final Thoughts

"No matter how bleak the chapter of our lives may look today, because of the life and sacrifice of Jesus Christ, we may hope and be assured that the ending of the book of our lives will exceed our grandest expectations."
 -"The Infinite Power of Hope", Dieter F. Uchtdorf, October 2008

      I recently sat in a Sunday school class where we talked about the story of Jairus in the bible. He was the man who came to Jesus and asked him to come and heal his dying daughter. On their way, Jesus stopped to help the woman with the issue of blood. While that was happening, Jairus' servant came and told him not to trouble Jesus anymore, because his daughter passed away.

      When Jairus tells this to Jesus, Jesus says, "Fear not: believe only, and she shall be made whole." (Luke 8:50). The people all knew she was dead, and yet Jesus went on to raise the girl from the dead.

      What seems too late to us, is not too late for God. No matter how much we think we might be messing things up for ourselves, I know that God can make things right, and He will as we choose Him. It might not go as we planned, or happen when we want it to. But God is merciful and loving, and His plan is that we return to Him full of happiness and peace.

      I can testify with confidence that marriage is not the answer to being happy and fulfilled- Jesus Christ is. I can be fully happy and fulfilled right now, and still desire marriage at the same time. I'm not a second-class member of The Church of Jesus Christ of Latter-day Saints because I am single. Maybe, God *needs* me to be single right now, and it's not a punishment. There can be joy and goodness and progression in my current state, even if other people can't see that. My path doesn't look like the path of most people around me, and yet that doesn't make me any less than anyone else. The same is true about you.

Your worth is not determined by a ring on your left finger. It isn't determined by the kind of job you have, or the house you live in, or the number of kids you have or when you have them. You are a daughter of God and that means you have infinite worth. No matter what trials come your way, no matter what crazy things life brings to you, know that as with Joseph Smith, ultimately and eternally all these things will give you experience and be for your good. You are amazing. You are enough. You are on the right track. You are worth more than rubies or diamonds. You are seen. You are priceless, and you are loved. You may be ringless, but you are oh, so far from worthless.

Did you find this book helpful?

If so, a review on Amazon is a fabulous way to help more people know this is a great resource.

Looking for more support and a tribe of awesome women?

Go to ringlessnotworthless.com or @ringlessnotworthless on Instagram to find resources, events, and more.

Elisa Black has over 10 years of experience as a YSA. Most of those years have taken place in Provo, UT. Some dating highlights include getting asked out in front of the Notre Dame Cathedral in Paris, accidentally grabbing a policeman's gun on a date, and having a blind date tell her he recently got out of jail as they were going on a walk late at night. She has been a bride's maid at least eight times. She has started three businesses, received a degree in musical theatre from SUU, been a foster mom, was a US representative for the International Women's Conference in Dubai, owns real estate in multiple states, and been a part of an A Cappella band. She served a full-time mission in Santa Cruz, Bolivia. Her favorite church callings during these years have been ward choir director, Sunday School teacher, and Relief Society teacher. She loves being the oldest of 6 children and adores spending time with her two nephews and two nieces.

Made in the USA
Columbia, SC
11 February 2023